COMPLETE BOOK OF
CHOCOLATE

COMPLETE BOOK OF
CHOCOLATE

LONGMEADOW
P R E S S

COOK'S NOTES

Use extra large eggs unless otherwise stated.

A number of recipes call for cake crumbs – use homemade or purchased yellow, white,
chocolate, or pound cake and crumble it finely between your fingers.

Where reference is made to a microwave, use a 650-watt oven with a turntable.

Cover design: Janet James
Interior design: Janet James
Cookery editor: Janet Smith
Editors: Helen Southall, Norma Macmillan
Photographer: James Murphy

ISBN: 0-681-00604-8

Typeset by Textype Typesetters, Cambridge
Printed by Tien Wah Press, Singapore

First Longmeadow Press Edition 1994

0 9 8 7 6 5 4 3 2 1

CONTENTS

INTRODUCTION

Chocolate is a consuming passion for many of us. Although nutritionists agree that its high fat and sugar content make it exactly the sort of food we should avoid, its unique, melt-in-the-mouth texture and inimitable flavor are irresistible.

Chocolate was probably first consumed as a drink, by the Aztecs in Central America, and it was introduced to Europe as such by the Spanish explorer, Don Cortes, in the sixteenth century. At different times in history, chocolate has been used as an aphrodisiac, a ceremonial refreshment, and even possibly as a currency.

Chocolate quickly became a popular drink in Spain, Italy, and France, but it was not until the end of the sixteenth century that it was introduced to Switzerland, now thought of as the chocolate capital of Europe. Finally, in the middle of the seventeenth century, chocolate became known in the coffee houses of London. The popularity of chocolate as a drink spread and new "chocolate" houses were opened, despite the fact that the heavy brew, thick with cocoa butter, tasted bitter.

In 1828, a Dutchman, Coenraad van Houten, discovered how to extract a large proportion of the fat (cocoa butter) from cocoa to produce a dry, powdery substance – what we know as cocoa powder today. Twenty years later, Joseph Fry, of Bristol, England, made the first eating chocolate by combining cocoa butter with chocolate liquor and sugar.

CHOCOLATE PRODUCTION

Both chocolate and cocoa are made from the cocoa bean, which grows in pods on the cocoa tree (botanically known as *Theobroma cacao*). These lush green trees originally grew in the Amazon Forests – they need moist, humid conditions and short dry seasons to flourish. Today, the trees are cultivated mainly in Africa, Brazil, and Malaysia; the beans are exported all over the world.

After harvesting, the large pods are split open and the pulp and seeds scooped out. This mass of beans and pulp is piled up on banana leaves and left for a week or more to ferment in the hot sun. During this time, the pulp becomes liquid and drains away and the beans begin to develop their characteristic chocolate flavor. After fermentation, the beans are dried and it is in this sun-dried state that they are exported.

Once inside a processing plant the dried cocoa beans undergo several more treatments until all that is left is a thick, chocolate-colored mixture known as chocolate liquor. This is then pressed, blended, refined, and conched (a process that pummels the chocolate backward and forward for several hours or several days). The end product of all this is chocolate as we know it.

In its purest state, chocolate is so bitter that it is virtually inedible unless blended with other ingredients. In this unsweetened form, it is traditionally included as an ingredient in several savory dishes, notably *mole poblano*, the Mexican specialty of turkey cooked in a sauce of chocolate, chilies, and nuts. In Spain, bitter chocolate is included in a sauce for spiny lobster.

TYPES OF CHOCOLATE

In these days of manufacturing wizardry, it's no surprise to find that chocolate comes in a variety of forms. The type of chocolate you choose will dramatically affect the way you use it, and the end result. There is no question that the more expensive brands, which contain high proportions of chocolate liquor, give the most intense flavor. These are the best choice when making special mousses or cakes. Other types have their own characteristics, as outlined below.

UNSWEETENED OR BITTER CHOCOLATE

This unadulterated chocolate contains 50–58 percent cocoa butter. As the name suggests, it does not contain any sugar. It gives a very strong chocolate flavor and is much used for baking, which is why it is also often called baking chocolate.

Unsweetened chocolate can also be purchased as *liquid chocolate*. This is convenient to use; however, liquid chocolate is made with vegetable oil rather than cocoa butter so it doesn't have the same texture and flavor as melted unsweetened chocolate.

BITTERSWEET, SEMISWEET, AND SWEET CHOCOLATE

To make these three types of eating chocolate, cocoa butter, sugar, vanilla, and lecithin are added to chocolate liquor in varying degrees. US standards require that bittersweet chocolate contain at least 35 percent chocolate liquor, semisweet and sweet 15–35 percent. However, the amount of sweetening added is not fixed but instead depends on the individual manufacturer's formula. In most cases, the three types can be used interchangeably in recipes.

Semisweet chocolate is also made into *chips*. These usually have a lower cocoa butter content than the 1-ounce squares or bars, so they melt less easily. They also taste less chocolatey.

MILK CHOCOLATE

This contains dried milk solids. Like other sweetened chocolate, the many brands of milk chocolate vary considerably, but the best contain higher proportions of chocolate liquor (10 percent is the minimum) and real vanilla. Milk chocolate is very sweet and creamy, and not as intensely chocolatey as bittersweet, semisweet and sweet chocolates, so it is most suitable for use as a topping or decoration.

WHITE CHOCOLATE

This is made from cocoa butter (rather than chocolate liquor), milk solids, and sugar. Avoid brands that contain vegetable oil instead of cocoa butter. They are confectionery coating, not chocolate. White chocolate will not set as solidly as dark chocolate and can be difficult to use. Take extra care when melting it.

COUVERTURE CHOCOLATE

If you want a really professional, glossy finish to confectionery and chocolate decorations, or a very intense "quality" chocolate flavor, then couverture, or commercial coating chocolate, gives the best results. It contains no fat other than naturally occurring cocoa butter and at least 32 percent of that. It will need to be tempered (see page 21) before use if you want to use it as a coating for confectionery or for decorations. However, if you're using it in a cake or mousse, or in anything where it is mixed with other ingredients, it can be used in the same way as any other chocolate. It is available in dark, milk, and white varieties, from specialty candymaking shops, wholesale bakery supply houses, or mail-order suppliers.

If you cannot obtain any couverture, use a good-quality semisweet or bittersweet chocolate that has a high cocoa butter content. Look out particularly for European brands of chocolate.

COMPOUND CHOCOLATE COATING

Also called imitation or chocolate-flavored chocolate, this is made from vegetable oil instead of cocoa butter and contains no chocolate liquor. It doesn't have the true taste of chocolate, so we do not recommend it unless specifically called for in a recipe. However, because it is a very stable and easy-to-handle product, we found that, when we mixed it in equal proportions with couverture chocolate, it was the next best thing to using tempered couverture for making confectionery and decorations. The emulsifiers and oils in the chocolate coating making tempering the couverture unnecessary. The disadvantages are that the flavor is less intense and the finish less crisp.

UNSWEETENED COCOA POWDER

Unsweetened cocoa is made from dried chocolate liquor ground to a powder. A small quantity imparts a strong, bitter chocolate flavor. The darker and richer *Dutch-process cocoa* is treated with an alkali, which helps to neutralize cocoa's natural acidity. This results in a more mellow flavor.

Cakes and desserts made with cocoa powder will not taste identical to those made with chocolate. This is because cocoa contains a relatively small proportion of cocoa butter (10–24 percent) and lacks the richness of chocolate. However, it is easier to work with since it does not require melting and is usually simply sifted with other dry ingredients or dissolved in a liquid.

Chocolate-flavored syrup is made from unsweetened cocoa and corn or sugar syrup, with flavorings, preservatives, emulsifiers. It should not be substituted for melted chocolate in a recipe.

COCOA/HOT CHOCOLATE

Cocoa mixes contain other ingredients such as milk powder and sugar. Some, often called *instant cocoa*, also contain lecithin, an emulsifier that makes it easy to dissolve the cocoa in cold liquid.

These mixes are unsuitable for cooking since the cocoa content is usually low and the flavor mild. Instead they are intended to be mixed with hot or cold milk or water to make a drink.

CAROB

Not truly chocolate, carob is made from the large, dark brown beans of the carob tree that grows in the Mediterranean area and the Middle East. The beans contain a sugary pulp that is dried and ground to produce a chocolate-colored powder or confection. It has become popular as a nutritious and healthy substitute for chocolate because it contains less fat than chocolate and no caffeine. However, it lacks the flavor and texture of the real thing and reacts differently when used in cooking. It should not be used interchangeably with chocolate or unsweetened cocoa in recipes.

IS CHOCOLATE REALLY BAD FOR US?

For most people, the pleasure of eating chocolate is frequently spoiled by a feeling of guilt. Is it really bad for us? Since chocolate contains high proportions of fat and sugar, it is exactly the sort of food we should all be cutting down on, and although it contains small amounts of calcium, iron, and the vitamins A and B, this is not enough to commend it nutritionally. It is worth noting, however, that the finer, darker, more expensive brands of chocolate (with a high chocolate liquor content) are lower in sugar and fat than cheaper brands. These specialist brands also have a stronger, fuller flavor, so there is a tendency to eat less.

Carob has a better nutritional profile than chocolate, since it contains less fat and sugar and no caffeine. However, most real chocolate lovers would agree that when it comes to taste, carob doesn't compare. Real chocolate deserves its place in the diet for pleasurable rather than nutritional reasons.

TECHNIQUES
WITH
CHOCOLATE

STORING CHOCOLATE

Both chocolate and cocoa quickly absorb other flavors and odors, and should be stored tightly wrapped in an airtight container in a cool, dry place. Before using in cooking, let chocolate come to room temperature, still in its wrappings or it will attract moisture. White and milk chocolates contain a high proportion of milk solids, so they do not keep as well as cocoa and dark chocolate.

Kept at a temperature of around 50°F, all chocolate should stay in good condition for about a year. If stored incorrectly (in too hot or too humid conditions), the cocoa butter or the sugar crystals in the chocolate may rise to the surface of the chocolate and become visible as "bloom" – a dull, whitish film. Chocolate that has developed bloom is still edible.

Plain, milk, and white chocolate can be frozen providing it is wrapped tightly and thoroughly so that no air can circulate around the surface of the chocolate. It should be thawed at room temperature, still tightly wrapped.

MELTING CHOCOLATE

Break or chop the chocolate into small, evenly sized pieces and put it in the top of a double boiler with any other ingredients as specified in the recipes. The bottom pan should be three-quarters full of gently simmering water. If you do not have a double boiler, put the chocolate in a clean, dry, heatproof, preferably glass, bowl and set it over a saucepan that's about one third full of gently simmering water. The bowl should fit snugly over the saucepan so that no steam can escape around the sides. The base of the bowl or top pan should not touch the water below. Heat the water gently but do not let it boil – a glass bowl enables you to see any tell-tale bubbles. Leave the bowl on the pan until the chocolate looks melted. Remove the bowl or pan from the heat and gently stir the chocolate until it is completely melted and smooth.

The temperature of the chocolate should not go above 122°F. If water or steam come into contact with the chocolate, the texture will be spoiled and the chocolate will "seize," that is turn into a solid mass that will not melt.

MELTING CHOCOLATE IN A MICROWAVE OVEN

Break or chop the chocolate into small pieces and put it in a clean, dry bowl. A glass bowl is best because it conducts the heat from the chocolate as it melts, and reduces the risk of over-heating. For small quantities, it is safest to use a LOW or MEDIUM setting. For larger quantities, and once you become more experienced, use HIGH.

The table below should only be used as a guide because melting times vary according to the brand and type of chocolate, the initial temperature of the chocolate, and the size and material of the bowl used. Check the chocolate frequently and prod it with a spoon – it may look solid when in fact it has melted. White chocolate will burn more easily so watch it very carefully.

Watchpoints

● Use a HIGH setting for compound chocolate coating (it will melt in less time than given in the table below).

● The addition of other ingredients, such as butter or liquid, will shorten the melting time.

Approximate melting times in a 650-watt microwave oven

QUANTITY	LOW	HIGH
2 ounces	5 minutes	2 minutes
3 ounces	5 minutes	2 minutes
4 ounces	5 minutes	2 minutes
6 ounces	6 minutes	2 minutes
8 ounces	6 minutes	2½ minutes

MAKING CHOCOLATE DECORATIONS

Chocolate decorations add the final embellishment to many cakes and desserts. Most can be made in advance and stored in the refrigerator or freezer until required.

LARGE CHOCOLATE CURLS AND CARAQUE

Spread melted chocolate in a thin layer on a marble slab or clean, smooth work surface, or the underside of a large, smooth baking sheet. When the chocolate is *just* set, push a clean stripping knife (a decorators' tool used for scraping off wallpaper) across the surface of the chocolate at an angle of about 25° (see above). If the chocolate doesn't curl, but breaks, then it has set too solid. Scrape it off and melt it again. We suggest that you buy a stripping tool and keep it only for this purpose. The side edge of a large, very sharp knife can be used instead but it doesn't make such large, fat curls. Smaller chocolate curls made with a knife are known as caraque.

To make two-tone chocolate curls, pipe or spread alternate lines of contrasting chocolate on the surface. Smooth with a metal spatula so that the lines of chocolate merge together. Proceed as above, working across the bands of chocolate.

The curls or caraque can be kept in an airtight container in the refrigerator, interleaved with wax paper, for at least 2 weeks (white chocolate) or about 4 weeks (dark chocolate). They can also be frozen.

SMALL CHOCOLATE CURLS

Using a large, thick bar of chocolate at warm room temperature (if the chocolate is too cold it will not curl) and a sharp swivel-type potato peeler, shave off curls along the length of the bar. For narrow curls, use one of the edges of the chocolate bar (see above); for fatter curls use the smooth, flat underside of the bar. If the curls crack as you shave them off, rub the edge or flat of the chocolate bar with your thumb; the heat from your hand should soften the chocolate sufficiently for it to curl without breaking. Store small chocolate curls in the refrigerator or freezer, interleaved with wax paper, until required.

Small chocolate curls are an excellent, last-minute way to decorate a cake or mousse, and they are much easier and less messy to make than large curls or caraque. They can be grated directly onto cakes or desserts; they are very easy to make once the technique has been mastered. Compound chocolate coating can also be used to make curls in this way and, with practice, it is possible to produce quite large curls.

CHOCOLATE LEAVES

Any well-defined, well-shaped leaves, free of chemical sprays, can be used for making chocolate leaves, though they must be clean, in perfect condition, and bone dry. Using a small paintbrush, paint the underside of the leaves with tempered couverture chocolate (see page 21) or one of the alternatives suggested on page 22, or with melted dark or milk chocolate. Be careful to avoid the chocolate dripping over the edge of the leaf or it will be difficult to peel the leaf off when the chocolate is dry. Leave the leaves on a wire rack in a cool place until set. (If you're in a hurry, put them in the refrigerator or freezer.)

If the chocolate layer on the leaf looks too thin, apply a second coat and let it set again. If making very large leaves, you may even need to apply a third coat. Carefully peel the leaf away from the chocolate (not the other way around).

To make two-tone chocolate leaves, brush a small amount of white chocolate on to the center of each leaf first (see above), then cover the remainder of the leaf with dark chocolate. Apply at least two coats.

Handle the chocolate leaves as little as possible as they very easily break in half or, if held for too long, will melt in the heat of your hand. About 8 ounces chocolate should make 45–50 chocolate rose leaves. Store the leaves in the refrigerator or freezer, interleaved with wax paper, until required.

PIPED CHOCOLATE SHAPES

Draw a series of simple outlines on a piece of wax or parchment paper. Turn the paper over. Temper some couverture chocolate (see page 21) or prepare one of the alternatives suggested on page 22, or melt some bittersweet chocolate. Cool the chocolate slightly so that it just coats the back of a spoon and stays there. If it runs off the spoon in a steady stream, it is not ready to use.

Spoon the chocolate into a small paper piping cone. Snip the tip off the cone and pipe the chocolate onto the paper, following the outlines. Let the chocolate fall slowly and evenly from the cone; do not try to force the chocolate out or work too quickly. Let set, then carefully lift the shapes off the paper with a metal spatula. Store in the refrigerator or freezer, interleaved with wax paper, until required.

Alternatively, pipe the chocolate in an irregular lacy pattern. Instead of marking shapes, drizzle or pipe the chocolate in freehand shapes onto a sheet of wax or parchment paper or foil. Let them set, then peel off the paper.

MODELING CHOCOLATE

To make your own modeling chocolate, melt 6 ounces chocolate (milk, dark or white) with 3 tablespoons light corn syrup. As soon as the chocolate has melted, remove it from the heat and beat the mixture until it leaves the sides of the bowl clean. Knead briefly and shape into a ball. Cover and chill in the refrigerator about 30 minutes or until the mixture is firm.

Roll out the modeling chocolate thinly on a work surface lightly dusted with confectioner's sugar. Cut out shapes as desired. Alternatively, break off small pieces and use like modeling paste to make leaves, flowers, and any other 3D shapes you desire. For a two-tone effect, combine white and dark modeling chocolate. To make strips of an even thickness for bows and garlands, or for draping over cakes, run the mixture through a pasta machine set on the thinnest setting.

To make chocolate berries, pull off small pieces of modeling chocolate and roll into small balls the size of cranberries in the palms of your hands. For very special cakes (such as the Chocolate Indulgence Wedding Cake on page 30), cover the berries with tiny pieces of edible gold leaf.

CHOCOLATE HORNS

To make eight chocolate horns, line eight cornu-copia molds with parchment paper. Melt 6 ounces dark, milk, or white chocolate (see page 12). Using a pastry brush, brush the inside of the paper-lined mold with a thick layer of melted chocolate, making sure that it goes right down to the tip. Chill until set.

If necessary, re-melt the remaining chocolate and repeat the coating as above. Carefully remove the chocolate-lined paper from the molds, then peel away the paper (see above). Store in the refrigerator or freezer until required. Serve filled with mousses, sorbets, or ice creams.

To make two-tone chocolate horns, melt 3 ounces each of dark and white chocolate. Brush half the inside of the paper with white chocolate and let it set, then brush the other half with dark chocolate. Repeat the layers if necessary.

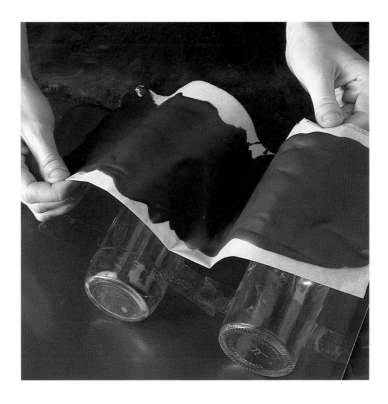

CHOCOLATE WAVES

Arrange two or three glass jars or plastic containers on their sides a few inches apart on a baking sheet and secure them with tape. Cut off a 14-inch strip of parchment or wax paper and fold it in half lengthwise. Spread the paper with a thick layer of melted chocolate and carefully lay it across the jars so that it curves up and down (see above). Freeze about 5 minutes or until set, then lift the paper off the jars and store in the refrigerator until required. Peel off the paper just before using to decorate cakes, mousses, desserts, or wherever a flamboyant chocolate decoration is required. Use a mixture of dark, milk, and white chocolate waves for a stunning effect, as on our Death by Chocolate cake (see page 34).

(To make striped waves, simply spread contrasting bands of dark, milk, or white chocolate on the paper.)

CHOCOLATE WATTLES

These unusual chocolate decorations reminded us of fencing made from interlaced twigs; hence the name.

Cover a rolling pin with parchment or wax paper, sticking it in place with tape. Temper some couverture chocolate (see page 12) or prepare one of the alternatives suggested on page 22, or melt some bittersweet chocolate. Cool the chocolate slightly so that it just coats the back of a spoon and stays there. If it runs off the spoon in a steady stream, it is not ready to use. Spoon the chocolate into a parchment paper piping cone and pipe lines of chocolate backward and forward across the paper. Chill or freeze until set, then remove the wattles from the paper and rolling pin and keep in a plastic box, interleaved with wax paper, in the refrigerator until required.

For an extra decorative effect, use wattles made from contrasting colors of chocolate together on the same cake or dessert. They can also look equally stunning dusted with confectioners' sugar or cocoa.

TEMPERING CHOCOLATE

The purpose of tempering is to make melted chocolate easier to use, especially for coating, and to produce a good glossy finish. The chocolate is melted, then worked until almost on the point of setting, then reheated to the ideal temperature. Tempered chocolate is not essential for any of the recipes in this book. However, if you want to make chocolate-dipped confectionery and molded candies, it is worth the effort. It really does make the chocolate much easier to handle and gives a professional result.

Tempered chocolate will dry rapidly at cool room temperature; it also shrinks slightly as it cools, so it should pull away more easily from a mold. When set, it will have an attractive high gloss finish that will last during storage. Untempered chocolate tends to become dull, streaky, or mottled if stored for any length of time.

There are several methods for tempering chocolate. The first step is to melt the chocolate. This can be done in the conventional way as described on page 12 or in a microwave oven. We found the latter to be the easiest and most convenient method.

1 Finely chop about 14 ounces of couverture chocolate and put it in a heatproof bowl. Microwave on HIGH for 2½ minutes or until completely melted. Stir with a wooden spoon; the chocolate should be very viscous. You should be able to see white streaks that look rather like oil on the surface. This is the cocoa butter in the chocolate and it is these particles that the tempering process aims to control. The temperature of the chocolate at this stage should be around 113°F (check on a thermometer, but providing the chocolate is fully melted, the temperature is not critical). Stir the chocolate in the bowl, then tip about three quarters of it onto a marble slab or a clean, dry, cool, smooth work surface. Using a flexible plastic scraper or metal spatula, quickly spread the chocolate out on the work surface, using a vigorous paddling or spreading motion to ensure that the chocolate keeps on the move all the time (see right).

2 Once the chocolate is spread as thinly as possible, scrape it up into a pool (see above) and start all over again. Keep repeating this action for about 5 minutes or until the chocolate no longer looks streaky and has cooled to about 82°F. Quickly scrape the chocolate back into the bowl with the remaining melted chocolate and mix the two together thoroughly. The temperature should be about 90°F. Use immediately.

To check if the chocolate is tempered correctly, put a little on the tip of a knife and let it set. It should set very quickly. If it doesn't set quickly, then it is not tempered, and the only thing to do is start again!

Watchpoints

● Always use couverture chocolate.
● Tempering is more difficult on a hot or humid day.
● Read the directions several times so that the method is clear in your mind before you begin.
● Cooling to the correct temperature is important.
● If the chocolate "seizes" into a ball on the work surface, it is because the surface was dirty or wet. You will have to start again.
● If you do not have a microwave oven, use the conventional method to melt the chocolate. We used the microwave because it is quicker and easier – this becomes especially relevant if more than one attempt at tempering is necessary!

Alternatives to Tempered Chocolate

If you do not want to go to the trouble of tempering, the following alternatives can be used for dipped and molded chocolates, and for decorations.

1 After tempered couverture, a mixture of couverture and compound chocolate coating gives the next best result, although the taste and texture is not as good as couverture on its own. This will never set to a crisp "snap" like tempered couverture.

2 Compound chocolate coating mixed in equal proportions with bittersweet chocolate. This will give a thicker coating and it will never set to a crisp "snap" like tempered couverture.

3 Good-quality bittersweet chocolate mixed with vegetable oil after melting, adding the oil a teaspoon at a time until it is the desired consistency. Don't add too much or the chocolate will not set hard. Chocolates coated by this method will require chilling in the refrigerator to set. Do not attempt to do this with animal fats or the chocolate will "seize" (turn into a solid mass).

4 Compound chocolate coating on its own. Use a good-quality brand.

CHAPTER ONE

CAKES

CHOCOLATE FUDGE LAYER CAKE

This gooey, three-layer chocolate cake is best cut with a large wet knife.

MAKES 12–14 SLICES

2 cups all-purpose flour
3 tbsp unsweetened cocoa powder
1¼ tsp baking powder
½ tsp baking soda
⅛ tsp salt
4 oz bittersweet or semisweet chocolate
10 tbsp butter, softened
1 cup light brown sugar, firmly packed
2 eggs, beaten
⅔ cup plain yogurt
½ tsp vanilla extract

For the fudge frosting
4 cups confectioners' sugar
1⅓ cups unsweetened cocoa powder
½ cup (1 stick) butter
6 tbsp milk

1 Grease three 7-inch layer cake pans, line the bases with wax paper and grease the paper.
2 To make the cake, sift the flour, cocoa powder, baking powder, baking soda and salt together.
3 Melt the chocolate (see page 12) and let it cool slightly.
4 Cream the butter and brown sugar together until pale and fluffy. Gradually beat in the eggs, then fold in the chocolate, the sifted ingredients, the yogurt, and vanilla. Turn the batter into the prepared pans and level the surfaces.
5 Bake in a preheated 375°F oven until risen and firm to the touch, 25–30 minutes. Unmold onto a wire rack and let cool.
6 To make the fudge frosting, sift the confectioners' sugar and cocoa powder into a heavy-based saucepan. Add the butter and the milk, and heat gently until the butter has melted, then beat until the frosting is smooth. Remove from the heat.
7 Use some of the fudge frosting to put the three cake layers together. Cover the sides and top of the cake with the remaining fudge frosting. Let it set.

ENGLISH MADELEINES

Not to be confused with French madeleines, which are baked in shallow, shell-shaped molds, English madeleines are baked in timbale molds, then coated in jam and coconut. They're traditionally made with a vanilla batter, but we thought this chocolate version made a pleasant change.

MAKES 10

½ cup (1 stick) butter or margarine, softened
½ cup + 1 tbsp sugar
2 eggs, beaten
½ cup + 2 tbsp self-rising flour
⅓ cup unsweetened cocoa powder
2 tbsp red jam, strained
½ cup dried shredded coconut (unsweetened)
Chocolate Butter Frosting (see page 152) and chocolate leaves (see page 15), for decoration

1 Grease ten timbale molds and stand them on a baking sheet.
2 Cream the butter and sugar together until pale and fluffy. Add the eggs, a little at a time, beating well after each addition. Sift the flour and cocoa powder together onto the mixture, then fold in, using a large metal spoon.
3 Turn the batter into the molds, filling them three-quarters full. Bake in a preheated 350°F oven until well risen and firm to the touch, about 20 minutes. Unmold onto a wire rack and let cool about 20 minutes.

4 When the cakes are almost cold, trim the bases so they stand firmly and are all about the same height. Melt the jam in a small saucepan.

5 Spread the coconut on a large plate. Spear each cake on a skewer, brush with melted jam, then roll in the coconut until evenly coated.

6 Top each madeleine with a small dollop of butter frosting and a chocolate leaf.

CHOCOLATE AND APPLE CAKE

This recipe for a genoese sponge cake, which is heavy with sweet apples, is made in the classic way. If you are in a hurry, you can cut corners with this particular recipe, because the weight of the apples tends to disguise the texture of the cake! Simply beat the eggs and sugar together with a wooden spoon, then fold in the flour mixture, followed by the melted butter, milk, lemon rind, and apples.

SERVES 6

1–2 tsp vegetable oil
1–2 tbsp dry bread crumbs
½ cup (1 stick) butter
4 eggs
⅔ cup sugar
1 cup cake flour
1 tsp baking powder
⅛ tsp salt
⅓ cup unsweetened cocoa powder
finely grated rind of 1 lemon
1½ lb Golden Delicious apples,
peeled, cored, and thinly sliced
confectioners' sugar, for dusting

1 Brush the inside of a 9-inch springform cake pan with oil. Sprinkle with the bread crumbs, then shake out the excess.

2 Put the butter in a saucepan and heat gently until melted, then remove from the heat and let cool slightly.

3 Beat the eggs and sugar with a heavy-duty electric mixer until pale and creamy, and thick enough to leave a trail on the surface when the beaters are lifted. (If using a portable electric mixer or balloon whisk, set the bowl over a pan of hot water while beating.)

4 Sift the flour, baking powder, salt, and cocoa powder into a bowl. Fold half the flour mixture into the beaten egg mixture with a metal spoon.

5 Pour half the cooled butter around the edge of the batter and fold in very lightly. Gradually fold in the remaining butter and flour alternately. Fold in very lightly or the butter will sink and result in a heavy cake. Fold in the lemon rind and apples. Pour the batter into the prepared pan.

6 Bake in a preheated 350°F oven until a cake tester inserted into the center comes out clean, about 40 minutes.

7 Leave the cake in the pan about 5 minutes, then unmold it onto a wire rack and let it cool completely, about 2–3 hours. Dust confectioners' sugar over the top of the cake just before serving.

RUM AND CHOCOLATE KUGELHOPF

This famous Austrian cake has as many variations in the spelling of its name as it does in the ingredients included. Basically, it is a rich yeast cake baked in a deep, fluted, ring-shaped mold. This version is a very rich mixture indeed, flavored with rum, fruit, and vanilla and filled with chocolate and poppy seeds. Because the dough is so rich, you need to add extra yeast to make it rise, so don't be tempted to reduce the amount given below.

MAKES ABOUT 20 SLICES

5 cups all-purpose flour
2 tbsp sugar
¾ cup golden raisins
½ cup chopped mixed candied peel
2 envelopes quick-rising dry yeast
1¼ cups tepid milk
3 tbsp dark rum
1 tsp vanilla extract
2 eggs, beaten
6 tbsp butter, melted

For the filling
⅓ cup poppy seeds
¼ cup dark brown sugar, firmly packed
1 tsp apple pie spice
2 tbsp butter
3 oz bittersweet chocolate

For the decoration
1 oz bittersweet chocolate
1 oz white chocolate

1 Put the flour, sugar, raisins, and peel in a bowl and mix together. Sprinkle in the yeast and mix thoroughly. Make a well in the center, then pour in most of the milk, the rum, vanilla, eggs, and melted butter. Beat together to make a very soft dough, adding the remaining milk if necessary.

2 Turn the dough onto a lightly floured surface and knead until it is smooth and elastic, about 10 minutes. Put the dough in an oiled bowl, cover with a clean dish towel, and let it rise in a warm place until doubled in size, about 1 hour.

3 Meanwhile, to make the filling, put the poppy seeds, brown sugar, spice, and butter in a food processor and process until smooth. Thoroughly grease a 3-quart kugelhopf mold.

4 Turn the dough onto a lightly floured surface and knead again about 5 minutes. Cut off one third of the dough and shape it into a thick sausage. Press this into the bottom of the mold.

5 Melt the 3 ounces chocolate (see page 12) and mix it into the filling. Spread over the dough in the mold. Shape the remaining dough into a sausage and put it into the mold on top of the filling. Press it down to seal the pieces of dough together.

6 Cover with a clean dish towel and let rise in a warm place until the dough has risen almost to the top of the mold, about 45 minutes.

7 Bake in a preheated 375°F oven until firm to the touch, about 35 minutes. Cover with wax paper to prevent it becoming too brown, if necessary. Let the cake cool in the mold about 10 minutes, then carefully unmold it onto a wire rack and let it cool completely.

8 When the kugelhopf is cold, melt the chocolates in separate bowls and drizzle over the cake. Let set.

DEVIL'S FOOD CAKE

This American classic is dense and rich. It is covered here with fluffy White Mountain frosting.

MAKES 16–18 SLICES

3¼ cups all-purpose flour
1 tbsp baking soda
⅛ tsp salt
1 cup unsweetened cocoa powder
1½ cups milk
2 tsp vanilla extract
10 tbsp butter or margarine, softened
1¾ cups dark brown sugar, firmly packed
4 eggs

For the frosting and decoration
3⅓ cups sugar
3 egg whites
2 oz bittersweet chocolate (optional)

1 Grease three 8½-inch layer cake pans and line the bases with disks of wax paper.
2 To make the cake, sift the flour, baking soda, and salt together. Mix the cocoa powder, milk, and vanilla together until smooth.
3 Using an electric mixer, cream the butter until it is pale and fluffy, then gradually beat in the brown sugar. Add the eggs, one at a time, beating very thoroughly after each addition. Beat in the flour and cocoa mixtures alternately. Divide the batter among the prepared pans.
4 Bake in a preheated 350°F oven until firm to the touch, about 35 minutes. Unmold onto a wire rack and let cool.
5 To make the frosting, put the sugar and ¾ cup water in a heavy-based saucepan and heat gently until the sugar has dissolved. When completely dissolved, bring to a boil and boil rapidly to 240°F. (Use a candy thermometer to check the temperature.)
6 Meanwhile, put the egg whites in a large deep bowl and beat until stiff. Slowly pour the hot syrup onto the egg whites, beating constantly. When all the sugar syrup has been added, continue beating until the mixture stands in peaks and just starts to become matt around the edges. The frosting sets quickly, so work rapidly.
7 Put the three layers together with a little of the frosting. Spread the remaining frosting over the top and sides of the cake using metal spatula. Pull the frosting up into peaks all over. Leave the cake on a wire rack for 30 minutes to let the frosting set slightly.
8 Melt the chocolate (see page 12), if using, then let it cool slightly. Spoon it into a parchment paper piping cone and drizzle it over the top of the cake. Let it set completely before cutting.

Opposite: Chocolate Indulgence Wedding Cake (page 30)

CHOCOLATE INDULGENCE WEDDING CAKE

This is a four-tiered chocoholics dream! Once coated with its shiny chocolate icing, the cake can be decorated as desired by the bride-to-be. For an autumn wedding, flowers and leaves in rich russet, gold, and brown tones would be perfect. Alternatively, embellish the cake with sheets of gold leaf (see page 17) or tiny white chocolate hearts cut from white chocolate modeling paste (see page 17), using a heart-shaped cutter. Tiny modeling paste balls coated in gold leaf also work well mixed with trailing ivy and flowers.

MAKES 100–120 SLICES

shortening, for greasing

For the 14-inch cake
2 lb bittersweet chocolate
2 lb (8 sticks) unsalted butter, softened
4½ cups sugar
1¾ lb (9 cups) ground almonds
20 eggs, separated
8 cups fresh brown bread crumbs
½ cup + 2 tbsp unsweetened cocoa powder, sifted
⅛ tsp salt

For the 12-inch cake
1 lb 2 oz bittersweet chocolate
1 lb (4 sticks) unsalted butter, softened
2¼ cups sugar
1 lb (5⅓ cups) ground almonds
14 eggs, separated
5⅓ cups fresh brown bread crumbs
½ cup unsweetened cocoa powder, sifted
⅛ tsp salt

For the 10-inch cake
10 oz bittersweet chocolate
1 cup (2 sticks) unsalted butter, softened
1 cup + 2 tbsp sugar
2⅔ cups ground almonds
8 eggs, separated
2⅔ cups fresh brown bread crumbs
¼ cup unsweetened cocoa powder, sifted
⅛ tsp salt

For the 8-inch cake
8 oz bittersweet chocolate
¾ cup (1½ sticks) unsalted butter, softened
¾ cup sugar
2 cups ground almonds
6 eggs, separated
2 cups fresh brown bread crumbs
3 tbsp unsweetened cocoa powder, sifted
⅛ tsp salt

For the glaze
1¼ lb (1¾ cups) apricot jam
6 tbsp liqueur, such as Cointreau or brandy

For the first chocolate icing
2 lb couverture or bittersweet chocolate
3¾ cups heavy whipping cream

For the second chocolate icing
1 lb couverture or bittersweet chocolate
2 cups heavy whipping cream
3 tbsp liqueur, such as Cointreau or brandy

1 Using shortening, thoroughly grease the pans and line them with wax paper. Make one cake at a time. Melt the chocolate (see page 12). Using a heavy-duty electric mixer, cream together the butter and sugar until pale and fluffy. Stir in the melted chocolate, almonds, egg yolks, bread crumbs, and cocoa powder and beat until well mixed.

2 In a scrupulously clean bowl, beat the egg whites with the salt until stiff. (When making the larger cakes, it may be necessary to do this in two bowls.) Fold half the egg whites into the cake mixture to soften it, then carefully fold in the remainder. Pour the mixture into the prepared pan and bake in a preheated 350°F oven until the cake is just firm to the touch: about 1¼ hours for the 8-inch cake (this is a slightly deeper cake so it will take longer to cook than the 10-inch cake), about 1 hour for the 10-inch cake, about 1½ hours for the 12-inch cake, and about 2 hours for the 14-inch cake.

3 Let each cake cool in the pan about 10 minutes, then carefully unmold it onto a wire rack and let cool completely.

4 Wrap the cakes in wax paper and foil and freeze until required.

5 When ready to assemble, make the apricot glaze. Warm the apricot jam with the liqueur until it has melted.

6 To make the first layer of chocolate icing, chop or break the chocolate into small pieces. Put it in a heavy-based saucepan with the cream and heat *very gently* until the chocolate has melted, stirring all the time. Remove from the heat and pour into a large bowl. Let cool slightly, then beat with a wooden spoon until the mixture is thick enough to spread. (On a hot day it may be necessary to cool it in the refrigerator.)

7 To assemble the cake, unwrap the still-frozen cakes and brush the apricot glaze all over the top and sides of each one. Spread a thin layer of the icing all over the tops and sides of the cakes, spreading it as smoothly as possible. Let set. (This will take about 2 hours – the icing will not set completely but should no longer feel sticky to the touch.) Reserve any leftover icing.

8 Put the largest cake on a cake board, then stack the remaining cakes on top, making sure that they are centered.

9 Stand the stacked cake on a cake-decorating turntable, if possible, or on a large wire rack or one of the smaller cake pans (upturned). Position the cake in the middle of a large work surface that allows you access to all sides of the cake if you're not using a turntable. Make up a second batch of chocolate icing, using any leftover icing with the chocolate, cream, and liqueur for the second icing. Remove from the heat and cool very slightly or until just thick enough to coat the back of a spoon.

10 Pour the icing into a measure, then pour it in a steady flow onto the top cake, letting it run all the way down to the bottom tier. If using a turntable, turn the cake around after pouring the first measureful to ensure that the coating is even. If not using a turntable, walk around the cake to do this, rather than attempting to turn the cake. The icing will run onto the cake board; make sure that this, too, is covered evenly. Try to avoid spreading the icing with a spatula because this will dull the shine. Let it set completely before moving.

11 When the icing has set, tie a ribbon around the sides of the board and secure with pins. Carefully position it on a cake stand or a second cake board. The cake can be kept like this for 2 days, although in the summer or when the weather is humid the icing will spoil if kept for more than a day. Add the final decoration of chocolate modeling paste balls or hearts, or gold leaf or chocolate leaves, or caraque, the morning of the wedding.

12 To serve the cake, lift the cakes off one tier at a time, using metal spatulas. Cut into thin slices with a large, sharp knife.

WHITE CHOCOLATE
WEDDING CAKE

This is a spectacular three-tiered concoction of light sponge cakes with a rich gooey chocolate-mousse filling covered in cream and masses of white chocolate curls. You will need three large round cake pans measuring 14 inches, 11 inches, and 8 inches. To assemble the cake, you will need two pieces of thick cardboard the same diameter as the middle and top tiers, and about 16 wooden chopsticks. Decorate the cake with fresh flowers to complement the bride's bouquet. Make the all-important white chocolate curls in advance and store in the refrigerator or freezer. The undecorated cakes freeze well and will thaw out overnight at room temperature. They can be decorated the night before the wedding and stored in a cool place (it doesn't have to be the refrigerator) overnight. It is easiest and safest to make and bake one sponge cake at a time. Do not attempt this recipe without an electric mixer, preferably heavy-duty. A very large bowl is also necessary, especially for the largest cake. To make a smaller version, omit the bottom tier and make just the middle and top tiers as below.

MAKES 60–80 SLICES

shortening, for greasing

For the 14-inch cake
14 tbsp butter
14 eggs
2 cups sugar
2½ cups cake flour
1 cup cornstarch

For the 11-inch cake
½ cup (1 stick) butter
8 eggs
1 cup 2 tbsp sugar
1¾ cups cake flour
¼ cup cornstarch

For the 8-inch cake
6 tbsp butter
6 eggs
¾ cup sugar
1¼ cups cake flour
¼ cup cornstarch

For the mousse filling
1½ lb bittersweet chocolate
½ cup brandy
8 eggs, separated
5 cups heavy whipping cream
4 tsp unflavored gelatin

For the decoration
5 cups heavy whipping cream
white chocolate curls made with
2½ lb chocolate (see page 13)
confectioners' sugar
fresh flowers

1 Grease the pans (see recipe introduction) thoroughly using shortening and line with wax paper.
2 Make one cake at a time. Put the butter into a saucepan and heat gently until melted, then remove from the heat and let stand a few minutes to cool slightly.
3 Beat the eggs and sugar with a heavy-duty electric mixer until very pale and creamy and thick enough to leave a trail on the surface when the beaters are lifted. (If using a portable electic mixer, set the bowl over a pan of hot water while beating.) As an approximate guide, the large cake should be beaten 25–30 minutes, the medium cake 15 minutes, and the small cake about 10 minutes.
4 Sift the flours and cornstarch into a bowl. Fold half of the flour into the egg mixture using a metal spoon. Pour half the cooled butter around the edge of the mixture and fold in *very* lightly and carefully or the butter will sink and the result will be a heavy cake. Gradually fold in the remaining flour and butter as before.

5 Pour the batter into the prepared pan. Bake in a preheated 350°F oven until well risen, firm to the touch, and just shrinking away from the sides of the pan: 1–1¼ hours for the largest cake, 40–45 minutes for the middle cake, and 30–35 minutes for the smallest cake. Unmold onto a wire rack and let cool. Wrap and store in the freezer, if necessary, until ready to assemble.

6 To make the mousse, melt the chocolate (see page 12), then remove from the heat and stir in the brandy and egg yolks. Whip the cream until it just stands in soft peaks, then fold it into the chocolate mixture.

7 In a small heatproof bowl, sprinkle the gelatin onto ¼ cup water. Stand the bowl over a pan of simmering water and stir until the gelatin has dissolved. Cool, then stir into the chocolate mixture. Beat the egg whites until stiff and fold in.

8 Cut each cake horizontally in half. Put the bottom half of each cake back into the bottom of each pan. Pour the mousse on top, dividing it proportionally between the pans. Chill until set. Put the second half of each cake back into its pan on top of the mousse, and press together. Carefully unmold the cakes.

9 For the decoration, whip the cream until it just holds its shape. Put the largest cake onto a cake board and cover with a thin layer of cream. Place the middle cake on a round of stiff cardboard (see introduction).

10 Push a wooden chopstick into the middle of the bottom layer of cake. With a pen, mark the stick about 1 inch above the top of the cake. Pull it out and cut it off with a Stanley knife, using the mark as a guide. Cut seven more chopsticks to the same height.

11 Insert the chopsticks in a ring into the bottom cake. Stand the middle cake on top to check that it stands level. Remove the cake, then repeat the procedure with the middle and top tiers, cutting eight more chopsticks to the required height.

12 Cover the middle and top tiers with whipped cream (do this on a board, not with the cakes in position). Cover all the tiers completely with the chocolate curls and dredge with confectioners' sugar.

13 Assemble the cake where it is to be served. (Do not attempt to move the cake once the tiers are in position!) Stack the tiers, one on top of another, and decorate with fresh flowers as desired.

DEATH BY CHOCOLATE

MAKES 24 SLICES

8 oz bittersweet chocolate
½ cup (1 stick) butter
1¾ cups sugar
½ tsp vanilla extract
2 eggs, separated
⅔ cup sour cream
2⅔ cups self-rising flour
1 tsp baking soda
For the filling
1 lb couverture or bittersweet
chocolate
1 cup (2 sticks) butter
6 tbsp brandy
12 oz white chocolate

For the icing and decoration
7 oz couverture or bittersweet
chocolate, finely chopped
⅞ cup heavy whipping cream
bittersweet, milk, and white
chocolate waves (see page 19)

1 Grease a 10-inch springform cake pan and line the bottom with a disk of wax paper.

2 To make the cake, melt the chocolate with the butter and ⅔ cup water (see page 12). Beat in the sugar and vanilla, then let cool.

3 Beat the egg yolks into the cooled chocolate mixture, then fold in the sour cream, flour, and baking soda. Beat the egg whites until stiff, then fold into the mixture. Pour the batter into the prepared pan.

4 Bake in a preheated 350°F oven until well risen and slightly shrinking away from the sides of the pan, about 1 hour. (The cake will have a slight crust.) Unmold the cake onto a wire rack to cool.

5 To make the filling, melt the couverture or bittersweet chocolate with the butter. Stir in 4 tbsp of the brandy and let cool until thick enough to spread.

6 Cut the cake horizontally into three equal layers. Don't worry if the middle layer has a hole in it (this will happen if the cake has sunk slightly); the hole will not show once the cake is assembled. Sprinkle the cut sides with the remaining brandy. Melt the white chocolate and spread it thinly over the three layers. Let set.

7 To assemble the cake, put the bottom layer back in the pan, white-chocolate-side up. Spread with half of the filling, top with a second cake layer, white-chocolate-side uppermost, and spread with the remaining filling. Put the final layer of cake on top, white-chocolate-side down. Cover and chill until set.

8 Carefully remove the cake from the pan and ease off the base. Run a metal spatula around the sides to make them smooth, if necessary. Set the cake on a wire rack placed over a baking sheet.

9 To make the icing, put the chocolate in a large heatproof bowl. Put the cream in a heavy-based saucepan and bring to a boil. (Watch it carefully because it will boil over once it reaches boiling point.) As soon as it reaches boiling point, pour it over the chocolate. Leave about 5 minutes, undisturbed, then whisk the mixture with a balloon whisk, starting slowly from the center of the bowl and gradually whisking more vigorously. The icing should be perfectly smooth and glossy.

10 Pour the icing over the cake, letting it run down the sides and using a metal spatula to help if necessary. Let it set (not in the refrigerator or the icing will be spoiled). When the icing has set, decorate with chocolate waves.

CINNAMON CHOCOLATE TORTE

MAKES 6–8 SLICES

6 oz bittersweet chocolate
¾ cup (1½ sticks) butter, softened
1 cup sugar
5 eggs, separated
1 cup all-purpose flour
2 tsp ground cinnamon
1 cup ground almonds
confectioners' sugar for dusting

For the filling
6 tbsp apricot jam
2 tbsp lemon juice
1 tsp ground cinnamon
1¼ cups heavy whipping cream

1 Grease and line two 7½-inch layer cake pans.
2 To make the cake, melt the chocolate (see page 12) and let it cool slightly.
3 Cream the butter and sugar together until pale and fluffy. Beat in the egg yolks, then add the melted chocolate with 3 tbsp water, mixing well.
4 Beat the egg whites until they stand in soft peaks. Sift the flour with the cinnamon and fold into the creamed mixture with the ground almonds and egg whites. Spoon the batter into the prepared pans.
5 Bake in a preheated 375°F oven until a cake tester inserted into the center comes out clean, 35–40 minutes. Unmold the cakes onto a wire rack and let them cool. Cut each cake horizontally into two layers.
6 To make the filling, melt the apricot jam with the lemon juice and cinnamon. Let cool. Whip the cream until stiff. Spread the apricot mixture on the cake layers and put them together with the whipped cream. Dust the top of the assembled torte with confectioners' sugar just before serving.

CHOCOLATE WALNUT LOAF

If wrapped in foil and stored in an airtight container, this loaf will keep 4 days.

MAKES 12–14 SLICES

¾ cup roughly chopped dried pitted dates
5 oz bittersweet chocolate
3 tbsp butter or margarine
1⅔ cups all-purpose flour
3½ tbsp sugar
1 tsp salt
1 tsp baking powder
1 tsp baking soda
1 egg
about ⅔ cup milk
1 tsp vanilla extract
1¼ cups roughly chopped walnut pieces
2 tbsp raw brown sugar

1 Lightly grease a 5- to 6-cup capacity loaf pan and line the bottom with wax paper.
2 Put the dates in a small bowl. Pour over ⅔ cup boiling water and let soak 30 minutes. Melt the chocolate with the butter (see page 12).
3 Mix together the flour, sugar, salt, baking powder, and baking soda.
4 Whisk together the egg, milk, and vanilla. Beat into the dry ingredients with all but 2 tbsp of the walnuts, the dates and their soaking liquor, and the melted chocolate. Spoon the batter into the prepared pan and level the surface. Sprinkle the reserved walnuts and the brown sugar over the top.
5 Bake in a preheated 350°F oven until a cake tester inserted in the center comes out clean, about 1¼ hours. Cool in the pan about 10 minutes before unmolding onto a wire rack to cool completely.

BATTENBURG CAKE

MAKES ABOUT 10 SLICES

¾ cup (1½ sticks) butter or
margarine, softened
¾ cup sugar
a few drops of vanilla extract
3 eggs, beaten
1 cup + 3 tbsp self-rising flour
2½ tbsp unsweetened cocoa powder,
sifted
milk
apricot jam
12 oz white marzipan or almond
paste

1 Grease and line a rectangular baking pan measuring 12×8×¾ inch and divide it lengthwise with a "wall" of wax paper or foil.
2 Cream the butter and sugar together until pale and fluffy. Add the vanilla, then add the eggs, a little at a time, beating well after each addition. When all the egg has been added, lightly fold in the flour.

3 Turn half of the batter into one side of the pan. Fold the cocoa powder into the other half with a little milk and spoon this batter into the second side of the pan.
4 Bake in a preheated 375°F oven until well risen and firm to the touch, 40–45 minutes. Unmold onto a wire rack and let cool.
5 When the cake is cold, cut each half in half lengthwise. Spread all the sides of the strips with apricot jam and stick each plain strip to a brown strip. Then stick one double strip on top of the other, so that the colors alternate. Press the pieces together well.
6 Roll out the marzipan thinly on a work surface dusted with a little confectioners' sugar, into a rectangle measuring about 14×10 inches. Wrap completely around the cake. Press firmly against the sides and trim the edges. Crimp along the outer edges and score the top of the cake with a sharp knife to make a decorative criss-cross pattern in the marzipan.

Overleaf: Battenburg Cake

CAPPUCCINO CAKE

This dark chocolate and coffee cake has a frothy cream and cocoa topping, reminiscent of a good cappuccino.

MAKES 16–18 SLICES

8 oz bittersweet chocolate
1 tbsp instant coffee granules
1 cup (2 sticks) butter or margarine, softened
1 cup dark brown sugar, firmly packed
5 eggs
1⅓ cups ground almonds
1 cup cornstarch

To finish
2 tbsp strong coffee, cooled
2 tbsp dark rum
1¼ cups heavy whipping cream
unsweetened cocoa powder, for decoration

1 Grease a 9-inch round springform cake pan and line the bottom with a disk of wax paper.
2 To make the cake, melt the chocolate with the instant coffee (see page 12) and let cool slightly.
3 Cream the butter and sugar together until pale and fluffy. Beat in the eggs, one at a time, beating well after each addition. Fold in the almonds, cornstarch, and melted chocolate. Pour the batter into the prepared pan and level the surface.
4 Bake in a preheated 350°F oven until risen and just firm to the touch, about 1¼ hours. Cover the cake with parchment paper to prevent it becoming too brown, if necessary. Let the cake cool in the pan.
5 When the cake is cold, prick it all over with a fine skewer. Mix the coffee with the rum and pour evenly over the cake. Let soak at least 30 minutes.
6 Whip the cream until it just holds its shape. Remove the cake from the pan and transfer it to a serving plate. Spoon the cream on top and spread it evenly with a metal spatula. Sift a little cocoa powder over the cream.

EGGLESS CHOCOLATE CAKE

This cake was created in response to requests for a cake made without eggs, suitable for vegans or those with an egg allergy. No one will ever guess that there's anything unusual about it! It's really moist, chocolatey, and irresistible. It also keeps very well, wrapped in foil or in an airtight tin.

MAKES ABOUT 12 SLICES

4 oz creamed coconut
⅔ cup unsweetened cocoa powder
2¼ cups self-rising flour
1 tsp baking powder
⅛ tsp salt
1 cup light brown sugar, firmly packed
⅞ cup sunflower oil
confectioners' sugar, for dusting (optional)

1 Oil and line a 7½- to 8-cup capacity loaf pan.
2 Pour 2¾ cups boiling water over the coconut and stir until it dissolves. Let it cool 30 minutes.
3 Sift the cocoa powder, flour, baking powder, and salt into a bowl and mix together with the sugar. Make a well in the center, then pour in the coconut mixture and the oil. Beat the ingredients together thoroughly to make a smooth, thick batter.
4 Pour into the prepared pan and bake in a preheated 350°F oven until well risen and just firm to the touch, about 1¼ hours. Let cool in the pan 10 minutes, then unmold onto a wire rack and let cool completely. Dust with confectioners' sugar before serving, if desired.

CHOCOLATE CRACKLES

MAKES 12

8 oz semisweet or milk chocolate,
broken into pieces
1 tbsp light corn syrup
4 tbsp butter or margarine
2 cups corn flakes or puffed rice
cereal

1 Place 12 paper cupcake cases on a baking sheet.
2 Melt the chocolate in a saucepan with the syrup and butter. Fold in the corn flakes or rice cereal, mix well, and divide among the cases. Chill in the refrigerator until set.

CHOCOLATE NUT MUFFINS

MAKES 12

4 oz bittersweet chocolate
1 cup roughly chopped Brazil nuts
1⅔ cups self-rising flour
1 tsp baking powder
¼ cup dark brown sugar, firmly
packed
1 cup milk
¼ cup sunflower oil
1 tsp vanilla extract
1 egg

1 Place 12 large paper cupcake cases in a 12-cup muffin tin.
2 Melt the chocolate (see page 12), then remove from the heat and quickly beat in all the remaining ingredients.
3 Spoon the batter into the paper cases and bake in a preheated 425°F oven until well risen and firm to the touch, 15–20 minutes. These are best served warm, straight from the oven.

DOUBLE CHOCOLATE MUFFINS

MAKES 12

4 oz bittersweet chocolate
⅔ cup unsweetened cocoa powder
1⅔ cups self-rising flour
1 tsp baking powder
¼ cup dark brown sugar, firmly
packed
⅛ tsp salt
⅔ cup semisweet chocolate chips
1 cup milk
¼ cup vegetable oil
1 tsp vanilla extract
1 egg

1 Place 12 large paper cupcake cases in a 12-cup muffin tin.
2 Melt the bittersweet chocolate (see page 12). Remove from the heat and stir in the remaining ingredients. Beat quickly together.
3 Spoon the batter into the paper cases and bake in a preheated 425°F oven until well risen and firm to the touch, about 15 minutes. Serve warm.

EXCEEDINGLY RICH CHOCOLATE BROWNIES

As the name suggests, these are very rich, fudgy brownies. Serve as a dessert with ice cream or whipped cream.

MAKES 24

1¼ lb bittersweet chocolate
1 cup (2 sticks) butter
3 eggs
2 tbsp freshly made strong coffee
1 cup + 2 tbsp sugar
½ cup + 2 tbsp self-rising flour
½ tsp salt
1½ cups chopped walnuts
1 tsp vanilla extract

1 Grease and line a cake pan measuring 8½ × 11½ inches across the top and 7½ × 10½ inches across the base.
2 Using a very sharp knife, roughly chop 8 ounces of the chocolate and set aside. Melt the remaining chocolate with the butter (see page 12) and let cool slightly.
3 Mix the eggs, coffee, and sugar together in a large bowl, then gradually beat in the melted chocolate. Fold in the flour, salt, walnuts, vanilla, and chopped chocolate, and pour into the prepared pan.
4 Bake in a preheated 375°F oven until *just* firm to the touch in the center, about 45 minutes. Do not overcook or the soft, fudgy texture will be ruined. Let cool in the pan.
5 When the cake is completely cold, turn it onto a board and trim the edges. Cut into 24 squares.

CHOCOLATE CUPCAKES

MAKES 12–14

½ cup (1 stick) butter or margarine, softened
½ cup light brown sugar, firmly packed
½ cup self-rising whole-wheat flour
¼ cup self-rising flour
⅓ cup unsweetened cocoa powder, sifted
a pinch of baking powder
2 eggs

For the chocolate fudge frosting
3 oz semisweet chocolate
2 tbsp butter or margarine
¾ cup confectioners' sugar, sifted

1 Spread 12–14 paper cupcake cases on a baking sheet or put them into tins.
2 Put the butter, sugar, flours, cocoa powder, baking powder, and eggs in a food processor and process until smooth. Fill the paper cases two-thirds full with the batter.
3 Bake in a preheated 375°F oven until well risen and firm to the touch, about 15 minutes. Transfer to a wire rack and let cool.
4 To make the frosting, melt the chocolate with the butter (see page 12). Remove from the heat. Add the confectioners' sugar and 2 tbsp warm water and beat well.
5 Spread the chocolate frosting over the cupcakes, working quickly before it sets. Leave to set.

Preceding page: Exceedingly Rich Chocolate Brownies

SPONGE CAKE

This classic fatless sponge cake does not keep well and should be eaten on the day it is made.

MAKES ABOUT 8 SLICES

3 eggs
7 tbsp sugar
½ cup + 3 tbsp cake flour
1 tbsp unsweetened cocoa powder
whipped cream, for filling
confectioners' sugar, for dredging

1 Grease two 7-inch layer cake pans, line the bottoms with wax paper, and grease the paper. Dust the insides of the pans with a mixture of flour and sugar.

2 Beat the eggs and sugar with a heavy-duty electric mixer until doubled in volume and thick enough to leave a thin trail on the surface of the mixture when the beaters are lifted. (If using a portable electic mixer, set the bowl over a pan of hot water while beating.)

3 Sift together the flour and cocoa powder. Sift half over the egg mixture and fold it in very lightly, using a large metal spoon. Sift and fold in the remaining flour and cocoa in the same way.

4 Pour the batter into the prepared pans, tilting the pans to spread the batter evenly. Do not use a metal spatula to smooth the batter as this will crush out the air bubbles.

5 Bake in a preheated 375°F oven until well risen, firm to the touch, and beginning to shrink away from the sides of the pans, 20–25 minutes. Unmold onto a wire rack and let cool.

6 When the cakes are cold, put them together with whipped cream and dredge the top with confectioners' sugar.

Variation

Chocolate Roll Make the sponge cake batter as directed but use ¾ cup + 2½ tbsp cake flour and 1½ tbsp cocoa powder and fold it in with 1 tbsp hot water. Pour the batter into a lined 13- × 9-inch shallow baking pan.

1 Tilt the pan backward and forward to spread the batter in an even layer. Bake in a preheated 400°F oven until pale golden brown and well risen, about 10 minutes.

2 Meanwhile, place a sheet of wax paper on top of a damp dish towel. Dredge the paper with superfine sugar.

3 Quickly turn the cake onto the paper, trim off the crusty edges, and spread with Chocolate Butter Frosting (see page 152) or whipped cream. Roll up the cake with the aid of the paper. Make the first turn firmly so that the whole cake will roll evenly and have a good shape when finished, but continue rolling more lightly.

4 Place the roll, seam-side down, on a wire rack and dredge with confectioners' sugar.

BÛCHE DE NOËL

Bûche de Noël is traditionally eaten in France at Christmastime. This and the English Yule Log date back to the days when a huge log used to be burnt on Christmas Eve.

MAKES ABOUT 8 SLICES

3 eggs
½ cup + 1 tbsp sugar
¾ cup cake flour
2 tbsp unsweetened cocoa powder
15½-oz can sweetened chestnut
purée

For the butter frosting
1 cup (2 sticks) unsalted butter,
softened
2 oz bittersweet chocolate
4 cups confectioners' sugar

For the meringue mushrooms
1 egg white
5 tbsp superfine sugar

For the decoration
holly sprigs
confectioners' sugar, for dusting

1 To make the meringue mushrooms, line a baking sheet with parchment paper. Beat the egg white until stiff, add half of the sugar, and beat again until stiff. Fold in the remaining sugar.

2 Spoon the meringue into a pastry bag fitted with a plain tube. Pipe the meringue onto the prepared baking sheet to resemble small mushroom caps and, separately, mushroom stems. Bake in a preheated 225°F oven until dry, about 1½ hours. Cool at least 15 minutes.

3 To make the cake, grease a 13- × 9-inch shallow baking pan. Line with wax paper and grease the paper. Dredge with a little sugar, then with a little flour, shaking out any excess.

4 Beat the eggs and sugar with a heavy-duty electric mixer until thick enough to leave a trail on the surface when the beaters are lifted. (If using a portable electric mixer, set the bowl over a pan of hot water while beating.)

5 Sift in the flour and cocoa and gently fold into the mixture. Fold in 1 tbsp hot water.

6 Pour the batter gently into the prepared pan and lightly level the surface. Bake in a preheated 400°F oven until slightly shrunk away from the sides of the pan, about 10 minutes.

7 Meanwhile, place a sheet of wax paper on top of a dish towel. Dredge the paper with superfine sugar. Turn the cake onto it. Trim off the crusty edges with a sharp knife. Roll up the cake with the paper inside. Transfer to a wire rack, seam-side down, and let cool 20 minutes.

8 To make the butter frosting, beat the butter until soft. Melt the chocolate with 1 tbsp water (see page 12), then let it cool slightly. Gradually sift and beat the confectioners' sugar into the softened butter, then add the melted chocolate.

9 Unroll the cold cake and spread the chestnut purée over the surface. Roll up again without the paper inside. Place on a cake board or plate.

10 Cut a thick diagonal slice off one end of the roll and attach it with butter frosting to the side of the roll.

11 Using a pastry bag and a large star tube, pipe thin lines of butter frosting over the log. Pipe one or two swirls of butter frosting to represent knots in the wood. Stick the meringue caps on top of the stems with a little butter frosting to form mushrooms. Decorate the log with the mushrooms and sprigs of holly. Dust lightly with confectioners' sugar.

CHAPTER TWO

LUXURY CAKES
AND
MERINGUES

CHOCOLATE-ORANGE MOUSSE CAKE

This delicious combination of a rich chocolate sponge cake topped with soft, chocolate-orange mousse is perfect for a dinner-party dessert.

SERVES **8**

8 oz bittersweet chocolate
1 tbsp orange-flavored liqueur
5 eggs, separated
⅔ cup sugar
½ cup (1 stick) unsalted butter,
softened

For the mousse
8 oz bittersweet chocolate
2 tbsp orange-flavored liqueur
4 eggs, separated

For the decoration
blanched julienne strips of orange
rind
grated chocolate

1 Grease an 8-inch springform cake pan, line with wax paper, and grease the paper.
2 Melt the chocolate (see page 12), stir in the orange-flavored liqueur, and let cool slightly.

3 Meanwhile, beat the 5 egg yolks and the sugar together with a heavy-duty electric mixer until thick and creamy. (If using a portable electric mixer, set the bowl over a pan of hot water while beating.) Beat in the butter, a little at a time, until smooth, then beat in the chocolate.
4 Beat the 5 egg whites until stiff, then fold into the chocolate mixture. Turn into the prepared pan.
5 Bake in a preheated 350°F oven until risen and firm, about 40 minutes. Let the cake cool in the pan 1 hour.
6 To make the mousse layer, melt the chocolate, then stir in the liqueur. Remove from the heat and let cool 1–2 minutes. Beat the egg yolks into the chocolate mixture. Beat the egg whites until stiff, then fold into the chocolate mixture.
7 Press the crust down on the baked cake with your fingers and pour the mousse mixture over it. Chill overnight.
8 The next day, remove the cake carefully from the pan and put it on a serving plate. Arrange strips of orange rind around the outside edge and decorate with grated chocolate. Keep in the refrigerator until about 30 minutes before serving.

BLACK FOREST CAKE

This famous and much-loved cake is from Germany. The cherries should really be fresh morello cherries, but as these are not always easy to come by, we've used canned cherries instead. When fresh morello cherries are available, poach them in a sugar syrup and carefully remove their pits before using them in the cake.

SERVES 10

6 tbsp butter
6 eggs
¾ cup sugar
1 cup cake flour
⅔ cup unsweetened cocoa powder
½ tsp vanilla extract

For the filling and decoration
2 × 15-oz cans pitted black cherries,
drained and syrup reserved
¼ cup kirsch
2½ cups heavy whipping cream
4 oz chocolate caraque
(see page 13)
1 tsp arrowroot

1 Grease a deep 9-inch round cake pan and line the bottom with wax paper.

2 To make the cake, put the butter in a heatproof bowl, place it over a saucepan of warm water, and beat until really soft but not melted.

3 Beat the eggs and sugar together with a heavy-duty electric mixer until pale and creamy and thick enough to leave a trail on the surface when the beaters are lifted. (If using a portable electric mixer, set the bowl over a pan of hot water while beating.)

4 Sift the flour and cocoa powder together, then lightly fold into the beaten mixture with a metal spoon. Fold in the vanilla and softened butter. Turn the batter into the prepared pan and tilt the pan to spread the batter evenly.

5 Bake in a preheated 350°F oven until well risen, firm to the touch, and beginning to shrink away from the sides of the pan, about 40 minutes. Unmold the cake onto a piece of wax paper on a wire rack and let cool 30 minutes. Cut the cake horizontally into three layers.

6 Place one layer on a flat plate. To make the filling, mix together ⅓ cup of the cherry syrup and the kirsch. Spoon 3 tbsp over the cake layer.

7 Whip the cream until it just holds its shape, then spread a little in a thin layer over the soaked cake. Reserve a quarter of the cherries for decoration and scatter half the remainder over the cream.

8 Repeat the layers of cake, syrup, cream, and cherries. Top with the third cake layer and spoon over the remaining kirsch-flavored syrup.

9 Reserve one third of the remaining cream for decoration and spread the remainder in a thin layer around the sides of the cake. Press on the chocolate caraque, reserving a little to decorate the top.

10 Spoon the remaining cream into a pastry bag fitted with a large star tube and pipe whirls of cream around the top edge of the cake. Top each whirl with a piece of chocolate caraque.

11 Fill the center with the reserved cherries. Blend the arrowroot with 3 tbsp cherry syrup in a small saucepan. Bring to a boil and boil, stirring, for a few minutes or until the mixture is clear. Brush this glaze over the cherries.

RIGO JACSI

Absolute temptation! These rich squares of chocolate cake, classic in their make-up of chocolate-flavored genoese and ganache, were named after a gypsy violinist, who was said to have broken the heart of many a princess.

MAKES 12 SQUARES

½ quantity chocolate genoese batter
(see page 52)

For the chocolate ganache
15 oz bittersweet chocolate
2½ cups heavy whipping cream
3 tbsp brandy

For the icing
4 oz bittersweet chocolate
2 tbsp brandy
1 cup confectioners' sugar, sifted

For the spun sugar (optional)
½ cup sugar
about 2 tbsp light corn syrup

1 Grease a 13- × 9-inch shallow baking pan and line the bottom with wax paper. Make the cake batter as described on page 52 and spread it evenly in the prepared pan.

2 Bake in a preheated 350°F oven until well risen, firm to the touch, and beginning to shrink away from the sides of the pan, 20–25 minutes. Let cool in the pan.

3 To make the ganache, break the chocolate into small pieces. Place the chocolate and cream in a large saucepan and heat gently, stirring, until the chocolate melts and blends with the cream. Do not boil.

4 Pour the ganache into a bowl and let it cool, but not set hard, stirring frequently to prevent a skin from forming. When cold, whip the ganache with the brandy until very light and fluffy, taking care not to overwhip the mixture.

5 Cut the chocolate cake across into two pieces. Place one piece in a deep square cake pan, placing it against two sides of the pan, then form a false "wall" for the other side, with several thicknesses of foil.

6 Spoon the whipped ganache on top of the cake in the pan and spread evenly to a depth of about 2 inches. Place the second layer of cake on top. Chill at least 1 hour.

7 To make the icing, break the chocolate into small pieces. Place in a small saucepan with 1 tbsp water, the brandy, and confectioners' sugar. Stir over a gentle heat until the chocolate melts and blends with the sugar to make a smooth icing. Spread the icing over the top layer and let it set.

8 Carefully remove the "wall" from around the cake. Cut the cake into 12 pieces, using a sharp knife dipped in hot water and dried each time before cutting. Chill until 20–30 minutes before serving.

9 To make the spun sugar, if using, cover a rolling pin with foil and oil it lightly. Have ready two forks tied or taped together back to back.

10 Put the sugar and ¼ cup water in a small heavy-based saucepan and heat gently until melted. Bring to a boil, then add the corn syrup. Half cover the pan and boil to 305°F. Immediately dip the base of the pan into cold water and cool 30 seconds only.

11 Dip the tines of the forks in the syrup and, holding the covered rolling pin in the other hand, flick the forks backward and forward over the rolling pin to form long strands of sugar. Repeat with the remaining syrup, then place on an oiled baking sheet. Use to decorate the cake just before serving.

CHOCOLATE AND CHESTNUT CAKE

For this stunning cake, thin rounds of chocolate sponge are layered with a rich brandy-flavoured chestnut cream. The easiest way to cut the cake horizontally into four layers is to set it flat on a board, then to slice through it using a large knife with a long, sharp blade. When putting the layers back together, make sure they are replaced in their original position, or you may end up with a lopsided cake.

SERVES 12

For the chocolate genoese
6 tbsp butter
6 eggs
¾ cup sugar
1 cup cake flour
2 tbsp cornstarch
⅓ cup unsweetened cocoa powder

For the filling and decoration
4 oz bittersweet chocolate
15-oz can unsweetened chestnut purée
1¼ cups heavy whipping cream
2 tbsp brandy
canned whole chestnuts, drained
grated chocolate
confectioners' sugar, for dusting

1 Grease a 9-inch springform cake pan and line with wax paper.
2 Melt the butter, then remove from the heat and let cool slightly.

3 Beat the eggs and sugar with a heavy-duty electric mixer until pale and creamy, and thick enough to leave a trail on the surface when the beaters are lifted. (If using a portable electric mixer, set the bowl over a pan of hot water while beating.)
4 Sift the flour, cornstarch, and cocoa powder together into a bowl. Fold half the flour mixture into the egg mixture with a metal spoon.
5 Pour half the cooled butter around the edge of the mixture and fold in very gently. Gradually fold in the remaining butter and flour alternately. Fold in very lightly or the butter will sink and the result will be a heavy cake. Pour the batter into the prepared pan.
6 Bake in a preheated 350°F oven until well risen, firm to the touch, and beginning to shrink away from the sides of the pan, 35–40 minutes. Unmold onto a wire rack and let cool.
7 To make the filling, melt the chocolate (see page 12) and pour it into a food processor. Add the chestnut purée, cream, and brandy. Blend until smooth, then turn into a bowl and leave a few minutes to cool and thicken slightly.
8 Carefully slice the cake horizontally into four layers and put them back together with a little of the chestnut cream. Cover the top and sides with the remaining cream and mark in a decorative pattern with a metal spatula. Decorate with the chestnuts dipped in grated chocolate. Dust the cake lightly with a little confectioners' sugar.

DOBOS TORTE

The old Austro-Hungarian empire is the home of this elaborate "drum cake." Versions of the traditional sponge rounds, layered with chocolate cream and glazed with caramel, are still to be found in the best cafés and pastry shops from Vienna to Budapest. Be sure to mark the caramel into portions before it hardens or it will be extremely difficult to cut.

SERVES 8

4 eggs
1½ cups sugar
1¼ cups cake flour

For the filling and coating
4 oz bittersweet chocolate
3 egg whites
1½ cups confectioners' sugar, sifted
1 cup (2 sticks) butter, softened
1⅓ cups crushed wafer cookies or
chopped nuts

1 Draw two 8-inch circles on two sheets of parchment paper. Invert the paper onto two baking sheets (so that the pencil marks are underneath).

2 Beat the eggs and ¾ cup of the sugar with a heavy-duty electric mixer until thick enough to leave a trail on the surface when the beaters are lifted. (If using a portable electric mixer, set the bowl over a pan of hot water while beating.)

3 Sift half the flour onto the mixture and fold in lightly with a metal spoon. Add the remaining flour in the same way. Carefully spread some of the batter out on the prepared baking sheets to fill the circles marked on the parchment paper.

4 Bake in a preheated 375°F oven until golden brown, 7–10 minutes. Loosen from the parchment paper and trim each round to a neat shape with a sharp knife. Transfer them to wire racks and let cool about 15 minutes.

5 Re-line the baking sheets with more marked parchment and spread on more batter. Bake, trim, and cool as before. There should be enough batter to make six or seven rounds.

6 Select the round with the best surface and lay it on an oiled baking sheet.

7 Put the remaining sugar in a small, heavy-based saucepan. Heat gently, without stirring, until the sugar has dissolved, then bring to a boil and boil steadily to a rich brown caramel.

8 Pour the caramel over the round on the baking sheet, spreading it with a knife brushed with oil. Mark into eight sections and trim around the edge.

9 To make the filling and coating, melt the chocolate (see page 12) and let it cool slightly.

10 Put the egg whites and confectioners' sugar in a heatproof bowl set over a pan of simmering water. Beat until very thick, then remove from the heat.

11 Put the butter in a bowl and beat until pale and very soft. Gradually beat in the egg and sugar mixture, then stir in the melted chocolate.

12 Put the remaining cake rounds together with some of the filling and put the caramel-covered one on top.

13 Spread the sides of the torte with the remaining filling and press the crushed wafer crumbs or chopped nuts into it to coat the sides.

CURLY WHITE CHOCOLATE CAKE

This rich cake, covered in a mass of white chocolate curls, is a scaled-down version of the wedding cake on page 32.

SERVES 18–20

9-inch baked chocolate genoese cake (see page 52)

For the filling
6 oz bittersweet chocolate
2 tbsp orange-flavored liqueur
2 eggs, separated
1¼ cups heavy whipping cream
1 tsp unflavored gelatin

For the decoration
¾ cup heavy whipping cream
large chocolate curls made from
1 lb white chocolate
(see page 13)
confectioners' sugar and
unsweetened cocoa powder, for
dusting

1 To make the filling, melt the chocolate (see page 12), then remove from the heat and stir in the liqueur and egg yolks. Whip the cream until it just stands in soft peaks, then fold into the chocolate mixture.

2 Sprinkle the gelatin over 1 tbsp water in a small heatproof bowl and let soak 2–3 minutes. Place the bowl over a saucepan of simmering water and stir until the gelatin has dissolved. Let cool, then stir into the chocolate mixture. Beat the egg whites until stiff, then fold in.

3 Cut the cake horizontally into two layers. Put one cake layer back in the pan and pour the mousse filling on top. Put the second cake layer on top. Let set.

4 When the mousse is set, whip the cream for the decoration until it holds its shape. Ease the cake out of the pan and cover with the cream. Cover completely with chocolate curls and dust lightly with confectioners' sugar and cocoa powder.

SACHERTORTE

Famous the world over, Sachertorte was the invention of Franz Sacher, a master sugar baker, in Vienna in 1832. It is a very rich, moist chocolate cake. This version is not entirely authentic, but it is the one we found most delicious.

SERVES 8–10

5 oz bittersweet chocolate
½ cup (1 stick) unsalted butter or
margarine, softened
½ cup + 1 tbsp sugar
1⅓ cups ground almonds
4 eggs, separated
1⅓ cups fresh brown bread crumbs
2 tbsp apricot jam, melted

For the icing
7 oz bittersweet chocolate
1 cup heavy whipping cream

1 Grease a 9-inch springform cake pan, line with wax paper, and grease the paper.
2 To make the cake, melt the chocolate (see page 12), then remove from the heat and let it cool slightly.
3 Cream the butter and sugar together until pale and fluffy. Stir in the almonds, egg yolks, bread crumbs, and melted chocolate, then beat until well combined.
4 Beat the egg whites until stiff and fold half into the chocolate mixture, then fold in the other half. Pour the batter into the prepared pan and level the surface.
5 Bake in a preheated 350°F oven until firm to the touch, 40–45 minutes.
6 Cover with a clean, damp dish towel, leave 5 minutes to cool slightly, then unclip the sides of the pan, and invert the cake onto a wire rack. Remove the base of the pan. Turn the cake the right way up, cover again, and let cool. When cold, brush the top with melted apricot jam.
7 To make the icing, break the chocolate into small pieces and place it in a heatproof bowl with the cream. Set the bowl over a saucepan of simmering water and heat until the chocolate melts and blends with the cream. Cool until the icing just coats the back of a spoon.
8 Set the cake and the wire rack on a baking sheet and pour over the icing. Gently shake the cake to spread the icing evenly and use a metal spatula, if necessary, to ensure that the sides are completely covered. Leave in a cool place to set, but do not put in the refrigerator or the icing will lose its shine.

CHOCOLATE-WRAPPED ORANGE LIQUEUR CAKE

For this unusual dessert, the cake is soaked in a liqueur syrup, and wrapped in an intriguing chocolate frill that is easier to make than it looks. Chocolate modeling paste (see page 17) works equally well.

SERVES 12

1 cup + 6 tbsp self-rising flour
½ cup cornstarch
1½ tsp baking powder
¾ cup sugar
3 eggs, separated
finely grated rind and juice of
1 small orange
7 tbsp sunflower oil
3 tbsp milk

For the liqueur syrup
⅔ cup sugar
finely grated rind and juice of
1 orange
3 tbsp orange-flavored liqueur

For the decoration
2 large oranges
1¼ cups heavy whipping cream
8 oz bittersweet chocolate
unsweetened cocoa powder, for
dusting

1 Grease an 8½-inch springform cake pan and line the bottom with wax paper.
2 Mix the flour, cornstarch, baking powder, and sugar together in a bowl. Blend the egg yolks with the orange rind and juice, oil, and milk, then mix into the dry ingredients.

Beat thoroughly with a wooden spoon to make a smooth batter. Beat the egg whites until stiff, then fold into the batter. Pour into the prepared pan.
3 Bake in a preheated 350°F oven until well risen and firm to the touch, about 55 minutes.
4 Meanwhile, to make the syrup, put the sugar, orange rind and juice, and ¼ cup water in a heavy-based saucepan and heat gently until the sugar has dissolved. Bring to a boil and boil rapidly 2 minutes. Stir in the liqueur.
5 Prick the hot cake all over with a fork, then spoon over the hot syrup. Let cool.
6 To make the decoration, peel the oranges, discarding all of the white pith. Roughly chop the flesh. Whip the cream until it forms soft peaks.
7 Remove the cooled cake from the pan and place it on a serving plate. Arrange the chopped orange on top. Spread the cream all over the top and sides.
8 Melt the chocolate (see page 12).
9 Cut a strip of wax paper long enough to go around the sides of the cake and wide enough to come 1½ inches above the top of the cake. When the chocolate has melted, spread it evenly all over the paper with a metal spatula. Let cool until no longer runny but still sticky when pressed with a finger.
10 Wrap the chocolate around the cake, pressing it gently onto the cream so that it sticks. Carefully pinch the chocolate and paper into loose pleats where it extends above the top of the cake. Leave until set, then carefully peel away the paper. Dust the top with a little cocoa powder.

CHOCOLATE TEMPTATION

The richest of chocolate desserts, this cake will keep in the refrigerator 3–4 days, during which time it will gradually become more fudge-like.

SERVES 8

9 oz bittersweet chocolate
1 tbsp instant coffee powder
2 tbsp brandy
4 eggs
1 tsp vanilla extract
5 tbsp sugar
2 tbsp cornstarch
½ cup unsweetened cocoa powder,
sifted
1 quantity Perfect Chocolate Ganache
(see page 152)
two-tone chocolate curls (see page
13) and confectioners' sugar, for
decoration

1 Lightly oil a 5-cup capacity loaf pan. Line the bottom and sides of the pan with parchment paper.

2 Break the chocolate into a heatproof bowl. Add the coffee powder, brandy, and 2 tbsp water. Place the bowl over a saucepan of gently simmering water and heat gently until the chocolate has melted. Stir until smooth, then remove from the heat and set aside to cool.

3 Using an electric mixer, beat together the eggs, vanilla, sugar, and cornstarch until very thick and pale. Fold in the cool, but not cold, chocolate mixture together with the cocoa powder.

4 Pour the batter into the prepared pan and bake in a preheated 350°F oven until a cake tester inserted in the center comes out clean, about 1 hour. (The cake may be cracked slightly.) Remove from the pan, place on a wire rack, and let cool.

5 Slice the cake horizontally in half and put the layers back together with two-thirds of the ganache. Spread the remaining ganache over the top and sides of the cake. Refrigerate 10 minutes.

6 Serve immediately, decorated with chocolate curls and confectioners' sugar, or wrap and store in the refrigerator up to 4 days.

STRAWBERRY-ALMOND LAYER CAKE

To make this dessert, a sponge cake batter is baked and, instead of being rolled up, is cut into three and layered with strawberries and cream. Make a Chocolate Roll (see page 45), then unmold it onto a sheet of wax paper dredged with sugar and let it cool.

SERVES 8

1 baked Chocolate Roll (see page 45)

For the filling and decoration
1½ lb small strawberries
1 tbsp confectioners' sugar
2 tbsp strawberry liqueur
3 oz bittersweet chocolate
2 tbsp strawberry jam
2 cups heavy whipping cream
a few drops of almond extract
1 cup sliced almonds, toasted

1 Hull and slice 1 lb of the strawberries and put them in a bowl with the confectioners' sugar and liqueur. Let stand about 20 minutes, stirring the strawberries gently from time to time.

2 Meanwhile, trim the edges of the cake, then cut acrosss into three equal pieces. Melt the chocolate (see page 12) and let it cool slightly.

3 Halve the remaining strawberries (leaving the stems attached). Dip the base of each piece of strawberry in the chocolate. Let set on wax paper.

4 Drain the strawberry slices, reserving the juice. Stir the jam into the juice and mix together. Brush a little of the jam and juice mixture over two pieces of cake. Top with the strawberry slices.

5 Whip the cream until it stands in soft peaks, then flavor to taste with a little almond extract. Spread a little cream on top of the strawberries.

6 Place the strawberry-covered pieces of cake on top of one another, then cover with the remaining piece of cake. Spread the top and sides with the remaining jam mixture, then cover completely with the cream. Press the toasted nuts onto the sides. Decorate the top of the cake with the chocolate-dipped strawberries.

MAKING MERINGUES:
YOUR PROBLEMS SOLVED

● For maximum volume, let the eggs sit at cool room temperature for 2 hours before using them.

● Egg whites should be beaten until they form stiff peaks – any further and water will seep out, leaving them dry so that they lose bulk, as they do if left to stand after beating.

● Traces of egg yolk or grease on the bowl or beaters will prevent the meringue reaching maximum volume and result in a runny meringue that won't pipe successfully. To ensure that the bowl really is greasefree, rub it with the cut side of a lemon.

● Insufficient beating before adding the sugar also results in a runny meringue. If beaten correctly, the whites should stand in stiff peaks that do not fall over at the tip.

● If the baked meringue is smooth on the outside with a hard, close texture, and very soft and chewy inside, or the sugar has bubbled out, the sugar was added too quickly or too much was added at once. If sugar weeps from the cracks, turn the meringue over onto a clean sheet of parchment paper and return it to the oven to dry out. This can even be done the following day.

CINNAMON MERINGUE FINGERS

These meringues freeze successfully. Pack them in a rigid container, with the layers separated by wax paper. Thaw about 2 hours at room temperature before filling with Perfect Chocolate Ganache.

MAKES ABOUT 18

3 egg whites
1½ cups confectioners' sugar
2 tsp ground cinnamon
1 quantity Perfect Chocolate Ganache
(see page 152)
confectioners' sugar, for dusting

1 Line three baking sheets with parchment paper.
2 To make the meringue, place the egg whites in a large heatproof bowl. Sift in the confectioners' sugar and cinnamon and set the bowl over a saucepan of hot water. Using a portable electric mixer, beat the egg whites and sugar until the mixture stands in very stiff peaks.
3 Spoon the mixture into a pastry bag fitted with a large star tube. Secure the paper to the baking sheets with a little meringue. Pipe about 36 fingers of meringue, about ½-inch thick and 3-inches long on the paper.
4 Bake in a preheated 200°F oven until dry, 2½–3 hours. Switch the baking sheets around during this time so that the meringues cook evenly. Cool on a wire rack.
5 Put pairs of meringue fingers together with chocolate ganache and dust with confectioners' sugar to serve.

CHOCOLATE AND GRAND MARNIER MERINGUE SHELLS

The raisins will slowly mop up the liqueur, giving them a delicious orange flavor. If you find it easier, use spoons to shape the meringues rather than piping them.

MAKES ABOUT 16

1 cup golden raisins
3 tbsp Grand Marnier or Cointreau
4 egg whites
1 cup + 2 tbsp superfine sugar
1¼ cups heavy whipping cream
7 oz bittersweet chocolate
confectioners' sugar, for dusting

1 Roughly chop the raisins and put them in a small bowl with the Grand Marnier. Stir well to mix, then cover and let them soak at least 4 hours.

2 Meanwhile, line two baking sheets with parchment paper. Beat the egg whites until stiff – the mixture should stand in peaks that just flop over at the top. Beat in 2 tbsp sugar, keeping the mixture stiff, then gradually fold in the remaining sugar.

3 Spoon the meringue into a pastry bag fitted with a ½-inch plain tube and pipe it in shells on the prepared baking sheets, making about 32 meringue shells in total.

4 Bake in a preheated 200°F oven until the meringues are well dried out, about 2 hours. Switch the baking sheets around halfway through the cooking time. Carefully peel the meringues off the paper, place on wire racks, and let cool. When they are quite cold, store in an airtight container until required.

5 About 2 hours before serving, pour 3 tbsp cream into a small saucepan. Whip the remainder until it holds its shape, then fold in the soaked raisins and any remaining Grand Marnier. Put pairs of meringues together with the cream mixture and pile in a glass serving dish. Grate over a little of the chocolate and dust with confectioners' sugar. Cover and keep in the refrigerator until required.

6 Meanwhile, to make the chocolate sauce, break up the remaining chocolate and add it to the cream in the saucepan. Pour in ⅔ cup water and warm gently until the chocolate melts, stirring occasionally. Simmer gently, stirring frequently, until the sauce thickens slightly about 3 minutes. Pour into a pitcher to serve with the meringues.

MERINGUE AND GANACHE CAKE

This very rich cake makes a lovely party-time special.

SERVES 14–16

4 egg whites
1 cup + 2 tbsp superfine sugar

For the filling and decoration
12 oz bittersweet chocolate
2 cups heavy whipping cream
2–3 tbsp brandy or rum
confectioners' sugar, for dusting

1 Draw an 8-inch circle in the center of each of four sheets of parchment paper. Place upside-down on separate baking sheets (so the pencil marks are underneath).
2 Beat the egg whites until stiff but not dry. Gradually beat in the sugar, a little at a time, beating well until very stiff and shiny. Divide the meringue equally among the prepared baking sheets, then spread evenly to fill the marked circles neatly.
3 Bake in a preheated 275°F oven until dry, 1–1¼ hours, switching around the baking sheets during cooking to ensure the meringue disks dry out evenly. Let them cool.
4 Meanwhile, to make the filling, break the chocolate into small pieces and put it in a large saucepan with the cream. Heat gently, stirring, until the chocolate melts and blends with the cream to form a smooth, rich cream. Do not boil.
5 Pour the chocolate cream into a bowl and let it cool, stirring frequently to prevent a skin from forming. When cold, add the brandy and beat well until light and fluffy.
6 Place one of the meringue disks on a flat serving plate, then spread with a generous layer of the whipped chocolate cream. Continue layering the meringue disks and filling.
7 Spread the remaining chocolate cream all over the cake to cover completely. Mark the cream into swirls with a metal spatula. Sift confectioners' sugar lightly over the cake. Put in the refrigerator until slightly chilled, but do not let the chocolate cream set too hard. Serve the cake straight from the refrigerator, still slightly chilled.

CHOCOLATE CHIP MERINGUE SHELLS

Serve these chocolate-speckled meringues with a bowl of fresh raspberries or strawberries, or a fresh fruit salad.

SERVES 6

4 egg whites
1 cup + 2 tbsp superfine sugar
4 oz bittersweet chocolate, grated
1¼ cups heavy whipping cream

1 Line a baking sheet with parchment paper.
2 Beat the egg whites until stiff but not dry. Beat in 4 tsp of the sugar, keeping the mixture stiff. Fold in the remaining sugar with the grated chocolate.
3 Spoon out 12 meringue shells on the prepared baking sheet, allowing them room to spread.
4 Bake in a preheated 250°F oven until dry, about 1½ hours. Peel off the paper and cool on a wire rack.
5 To serve, whip the cream until softly stiff and use to put pairs of meringues together.

CHOCOLATE AND CHESTNUT MERINGUE CAKE

The meringues can be made in advance and stored in an airtight container. Do not layer them with the filling more than 2 hours before serving or they will become soggy.

SERVES 10–12

1¼ cups shelled hazelnuts
6 egg whites
1¾ cups superfine sugar

For the filling and decoration
8 oz bittersweet chocolate
¼ cup dark rum
1⅓ cups canned sweetened chestnut purée
1¼ cups heavy whipping cream
toasted and chopped hazelnuts, for decoration

1 Grease three 8-inch round layer cake pans and line the bottom with wax paper.
2 Toast the hazelnuts lightly under the broiler, shaking the pan frequently. Transfer the nuts to a clean dish towel and rub gently while still hot to remove the skins. Grind until very fine.
3 Put the egg whites in a large bowl and beat until very stiff and standing in peaks. Beat in half of the sugar and continue beating until the meringue is glossy. Fold in the remaining sugar with the hazelnuts.
4 Divide the meringue among the prepared cake pans. Level the tops and bake in a preheated 350°F oven until crisp, 35–40 minutes.
5 Invert the pans on a wire rack and unmold the meringue disks. Peel off the lining papers carefully. (Don't worry if the meringues are cracked.) Let cool.
6 To make the filling, melt the chocolate with the rum (see page 12). Remove from the heat and gradually blend in 1 cup of the chestnut purée.
7 Put one meringue disk, soft-side uppermost, on a serving plate. Spread with half of the chocolate and chestnut mixture, then top with the second meringue disk, crisp side uppermost. Spread with the remaining mixture, then top with the last disk, crisp side uppermost.
8 Whip the cream until it holds its shape. Reserve 2 tbsp of the cream and swirl the remainder all over the cake to cover the top and sides completely. Blend the remaining chestnut purée into the reserved cream, then pipe around the top edge of the cake. Decorate with hazelnuts. Chill in the refrigerator before serving.

CHOCOLATE PAVLOVA

A luscious meringue base, topped with cream and a huge pile of chocolate curls. For sheer decadence, add a layer of whipped Perfect Chocolate Ganache (see page 152) before the layer of cream and top the chocolate curls with chocolate-dipped strawberries and a few red currants.

SERVES 8–10

3 egg whites
¾ cup superfine sugar
1 tsp cornstarch
1 tsp white wine vinegar
¾ cup heavy whipping cream
1¼ cups thick plain yogurt
12 oz dark and white chocolate
curls (see page 13), or grated
chocolate
confectioners' sugar, for dusting

1 Draw a 9-inch oval on a piece of parchment paper and place upside-down on a baking sheet.

2 Beat the egg whites until very stiff. Add one third of the sugar and continue beating until stiff again. Add another third of the sugar and beat again. Add the remaining sugar and continue beating until the meringue forms soft peaks. Fold in the cornstarch and vinegar.

3 Pile or pipe the meringue into the oval marked on the baking sheet. Make a hollow in the center to hold the filling.

4 Bake in a preheated 350°F oven for 5 minutes, then reduce the oven temperature to 250°F and continue baking until the meringue is set but still soft in the middle, 45–50 minutes longer.

5 Let cool slightly, then carefully peel off the paper. Don't worry if the meringue cracks a little at this stage. Let it cool completely.

6 Whip the cream until it just holds its shape, then fold in the yogurt. Pile on top of the Pavlova and sprinkle with the chocolate curls. Dust the top of the Pavlova with confectioners' sugar.

CHOCOLATE MERINGUE ROULADE

This meringue mixture is baked like a jelly roll, then filled with cream, chocolate, and fruit. Perfect Chocolate Ganache (see page 152), thinned with a little cream or milk, could also be used as a filling, or serve the roulade with a hot chocolate sauce (see page 153).

SERVES 6

4 egg whites
1 cup + 2 tbsp superfine sugar
⅔ cup heavy whipping cream
confectioners' sugar, for dusting
4 oz bittersweet or milk chocolate, coarsely grated
8 oz raspberries, strawberries, or a mixture of fresh fruit, prepared as necessary
unsweetened cocoa powder, for dusting
whipped cream and bittersweet or milk chocolate caraque (see page 13), for decoration

1 First prepare the paper case. Cut out two sheets of parchment paper, each measuring 12 × 15 inches. Place together, then fold up 1 inch all around and snip into the corners. Fold the corners around and pin or staple together, forming a strong, double-thickness rectangular paper case. Place on a baking sheet.

2 Beat the egg whites until they stand in soft peaks. Beat in half of the sugar, adding about 2 tbsp at a time and beating thoroughly between each addition so the mixture remains stiff. Fold in the remaining sugar.

3 Spoon the meringue into the paper case, spreading it gently and evenly into the corners.

4 Bake the meringue in a preheated 200°F oven until it is just tinged with color and firm yet spongy when lightly pressed, 40–45 minutes. Let cool about 1 hour. Whip the cream until it just holds its shape.

5 Place a large sheet of parchment paper on a work surface and dust it with confectioners' sugar. Snip open the corners of the paper case and ease the paper away from the meringue using a blunt knife. Flip the meringue onto the parchment and carefully peel away the paper case. If the meringue sticks, gently scrape it away with the knife and patch it up as necessary.

6 Spread the cream over the meringue and sprinkle with the grated chocolate and the fruit. Roll up the meringue from one of the narrow ends, using the paper to help. It will crack a little as it is rolled. Slide it onto a flat serving platter. Dust with cocoa powder and decorate with piped whipped cream and chocolate caraque. Cover loosely and keep in the refrigerator for up to 4 hours before serving.

BROWN SUGAR-PECAN MERINGUE CAKE

Chop the nuts roughly, by hand. If they are chopped too finely in a food processor, we found that they spoiled the texture and volume of the meringue.

SERVES 8–10

4 egg whites
½ cup + 1 tbsp superfine sugar
½ cup light brown sugar, firmly packed
1 cup roughly chopped, toasted pecans

For the filling and decoration
4 oz bittersweet chocolate
2 cups heavy whipping cream
confectioners' sugar and unsweetened cocoa powder, for dusting

1 Draw a 9-inch circle on each of two sheets of parchment paper. Place the paper upside-down on two baking sheets (so that the pencil marks are underneath).

2 Beat the egg whites until they stand in soft peaks. Mix together the sugars and add to the egg whites, beating in about 1 tbsp at a time. Beat well between each addition until the mixture is stiff. Fold in about three-quarters of the nuts.

3 Spread the meringue mixture in the circles marked on the parchment paper. Sprinkle the remaining chopped nuts over one meringue.

4 Bake in a preheated 300°F oven until the meringue is just set and firm to the touch, about 1½ hours. When quite cold, peel off the paper.

5 Meanwhile, prepare the filling. Break up the chocolate and place it in a small saucepan with ⅔ cup of the cream. Warm gently until the chocolate melts, stirring occasionally. Bring to a boil, stirring, then remove from the heat. Cool, cover, and refrigerate until required.

6 About 1 hour before using, remove the chocolate filling from the refrigerator and let it soften, then carefully spread it over the plain meringue disk. Whip the remaining cream and spread it over the chocolate. Finish with the nut-topped meringue disk. Refrigerate 2–3 hours before serving, dusted with confectioners' sugar and cocoa powder.

CRISP CHOCOLATE MERINGUE CAKES

These rounds of meringue are coated with a layer of chocolate and filled with fruit and cream.

SERVES 6

3 egg whites
¾ cup superfine sugar
6 oz bittersweet or milk chocolate
1¼ cups heavy whipping cream
12 oz fresh fruit of your choice,
prepared as necessary
unsweetened cocoa powder, for
dredging
piped chocolate shapes
(see page 16), for decoration
Coffee Custard Sauce (see page 153),
for serving (optional)

1 Mark twelve 3½-inch circles on two sheets of parchment paper. Place upside-down on two baking sheets (so the pencil marks are underneath).

2 Beat the egg whites until stiff, then beat in half of the sugar. Carefully fold in the remaining sugar with a metal spoon. Spoon the mixture into a pastry bag fitted with a large star tube and pipe on the paper, using the circles as a guide.

3 Bake in a preheated 250°F oven about 1½ hours if you like soft meringues, or 2½–3 hours for crisp, dry meringues. Let cool slightly, then carefully peel off the paper, place the meringues on a wire rack, and let them cool completely.

4 Melt the chocolate (see page 12) and let it cool slightly, then spread over the under-sides of the meringues. Return to the wire rack and let set.

5 Whip the cream until it just holds its shape. Pipe or spread a little of it on six of the meringue disks (on top of the choc-olate). Top with one of the remaining meringue disks, chocolate-side down.

6 Spread the meringues with more cream and top with the prepared fruit. Dredge with cocoa powder and decorate with chocolate shapes. Serve each meringue on a pool of Coffee Custard Sauce, if liked.

CHAPTER THREE

HOT DESSERTS

CHOCOLATE PHYLLO PIE

An unusual but delicious way to use up stale cake crumbs.

SERVES 9–12

*4 large sheets of phyllo pastry,
thawed if frozen*
4 tbsp butter, melted

For the filling
6 tbsp butter, softened
¾ cup confectioners' icing sugar
4 eggs, separated
1 cup ground almonds
*2⅓ cups white or chocolate cake
crumbs*
¾ cup dried mixed fruit
4 oz bittersweet chocolate, grated
*1 tbsp unsweetened cocoa powder,
sifted*
⅔ cup heavy whipping cream

For the decoration
⅔ cup sliced almonds
1 tbsp confectioners' sugar, sifted

1 To make the filling, cream the butter and confectioners' sugar together until pale and fluffy. Gradually beat in the egg yolks, then the almonds, cake crumbs, mixed fruit, chocolate, cocoa powder, and cream. Beat the egg whites until stiff, then fold into the chocolate mixture.

2 Fold one sheet of phyllo pastry in half and trim to fit an (8½- × 11½-inch) baking dish. Repeat with the remaining sheets of pastry, reserving the trimmings.

3 Lay one of the folded sheets of pastry in the dish and spread with one-third of the chocolate filling. Cover with a second folded sheet of pastry. Repeat the layers twice more, ending with a pastry layer. Brush the top with the melted butter. Cut the pastry trimmings into neat strips and sprinkle on top. Brush with more melted butter and sprinkle with the almonds and confectioners' sugar.

4 Bake in a preheated 375°F oven until golden brown, about 40 minutes. Serve hot or cold, cut into squares, with vanilla ice cream.

BAKED CHOCOLATE MARBLE PUDDING

A delicious family dessert to serve on cold winter days.

SERVES 8

3 oz bittersweet chocolate
*¾ cup (1½ sticks) butter or
margarine, softened*
*¾ cup light brown sugar, firmly
packed*
3 eggs, beaten
1 cup + 6 tbsp self-rising flour
3 tbsp milk
2 oz macaroons

1 Grease a 6-cup capacity loaf dish.

2 Melt the chocolate (see page 12) and let it cool (but not set).

3 Meanwhile, cream the butter and sugar together until pale and fluffy. Gradually beat in the eggs, beating well after each addition, then fold in the flour and milk.

4 Divide the batter in half and flavor one half with the melted chocolate, folding it evenly through the batter.

5 Place alternate spoonfuls of the batters in two layers in the prepared dish and zig-zag a knife through the mixture to create a marbled pattern. Roughly crush the macaroons and scatter them over the top. Cover with foil.

6 Bake in a preheated 350°F oven until firm to the touch, about 1¼ hours. Unmold and serve thickly sliced with Chocolate Custard Sauce or Chocolate Fudge Sauce (see page 153).

CHOCOLATE CINNAMON CRÊPES

This makes ten generously filled crêpes, enough for five, allowing two each.

SERVES 5

¾ cup all-purpose flour
⅛ tsp salt
2 tsp ground cinnamon
1 egg
1¼ cups milk
oil for frying
grated white and dark chocolate,
for decoration

For the filling
¾ cup all-purpose flour
5 tbsp sugar
1 tsp ground cinnamon
1¼ cups milk
2 oz bittersweet chocolate, chopped
grated rind of 1 lemon
4 eggs, separated

1 Sift the flour, salt, and cinnamon into a bowl and make a well in the center. Break in the egg and beat well with a wooden spoon. Gradually beat in the milk, drawing in the flour from the sides to make a smooth batter.
2 Heat a little oil in a 7-inch crêpe pan, tipping it around the bottom and sides of the pan, until hot. Pour off any surplus oil.
3 Pour in just enough batter to coat the bottom of the pan thinly. Cook until golden brown underneath, 1–2 minutes. Turn or toss and cook the second side until golden.
4 Transfer the crêpe to a plate and keep hot. Repeat with the remaining batter to make ten crêpes. Pile the cooked crêpes on top of each other, with wax paper in between each one, and keep warm in the oven while cooking the remainder.
5 To make the filling, mix the flour, sugar, and cinnamon together in a bowl. Blend to a smooth paste with a little of the milk. Heat the remaining milk to boiling point and whisk in the flour mixture. Bring to a boil, whisking all the time until very thick. Remove from the heat.
6 Stir the chocolate and lemon rind into the mixture until completely blended and smooth. Gradually beat in the egg yolks. Beat the egg whites until stiff, then fold into the mixture.
7 Spoon about ¼ cup of the filling mixture on the center of each crêpe. Fold in the sides to enclose completely. Arrange the crêpes, seam-side downward, in a single layer in a greased ovenproof dish.
8 Bake in a preheated 425°F oven until the filling is just set, 15–20 minutes. Serve hot or cold, decorated with grated white and dark chocolate.

FRESH FRUIT WITH HOT CHOCOLATE AND CREAMY FUDGE DIPS

Keep the dips hot over simmering water until you're ready to serve.

SERVES 6–8

2 oz fudge-filled chocolate candy bars
6 tbsp light whipping cream
4 oz semisweet chocolate
1 tbsp butter
prepared fresh fruits, such as seedless grapes, pineapple, bananas, apples, pears
cream or chocolate, for decoration

1 For the Creamy Fudge Dip, break the fudge-filled chocolate candy bars into small pieces and place in a small heatproof bowl. Add the cream. Place over a saucepan of gently simmering water until completely melted, stirring occasionally until smooth.
2 For the Hot Chocolate Dip, melt the semisweet chocolate with 3 tbsp water (see page 12). Add the butter and stir until smooth.
3 Arrange the prepared fruits around the edge of a large platter. Place the Hot Chocolate and Creamy Fudge Dips in the center. Decorate the surfaces of the dips with swirls of cream or grated chocolate. Serve immediately.

UPSIDE-DOWN PEAR PUDDING

SERVES 8

10 oz semisweet chocolate
½ cup (1 stick) butter or margarine
2 eggs
7 tbsp sugar
½ tsp vanilla extract
1 tbsp strong black coffee
½ cup + 2 tbsp self-rising flour
¾ cup roughly chopped pecans
1½ lb ripe pears or 2 ×
16-oz cans pear quarters, drained

1 Grease a 9-inch round ovenproof dish (5-cup capacity) and line the bottom with parchment paper. Roughly chop 3 ounces of the chocolate. Melt the remaining chocolate with the butter (see page 12), then remove from the heat and let cool slightly.
2 Beat together the eggs, sugar, vanilla, coffee, and melted chocolate. Fold in the flour, chopped chocolate, and nuts, and mix well.
3 Peel, quarter, and core the pears and arrange them in the prepared dish. Pour over the chocolate mixture.
4 Bake in a preheated 375°F oven 1 hour, covering with foil after 30 minutes. Cool slightly, then unmold onto a plate and serve with ice cream.

Opposite: Upside-Down Pear Pudding

INDIVIDUAL CHOCOLATE-MINT SOUFFLÉS

For added luxury, pour in a little cream when serving.

SERVES 4–6

⅔ cup milk
12 After Eight mints
2 tbsp butter or margarine
2½ tbsp all-purpose flour
2 tbsp sugar
3 eggs, separated

1 Lightly grease six ¾-cup capacity ramekin dishes.
2 Heat the milk and mints in a saucepan until melted and evenly blended.
3 Melt the butter in a large heavy-based saucepan. Add the flour and cook 1 minute, then remove from the heat and gradually blend in the milk and mint mixture. Bring to a boil, stirring all the time, and cook 1 minute.
4 Let cool slightly, then beat in the sugar and egg yolks.
5 Beat the egg whites until stiff but not dry. Beat one spoonful into the sauce to lighten it, then carefully fold in the remaining egg white. Spoon into the prepared dishes. Stand the dishes on a baking sheet.
6 Bake in a preheated 375°F oven until lightly set, 15–20 minutes. Serve immediately.

CHOCOLATE-CINNAMON SOUFFLÉ

If you like a soufflé to be soft in the middle, bake it for the minimum time given here; if you prefer it set throughout, bake at least 40 minutes.

SERVES 4

3 oz semisweet chocolate
¼ cups + 1 tbsp milk
4 tbsp butter or margarine
5 tbsp all-purpose flour
½ tsp ground cinnamon
5 eggs, separated
2 tbsp sugar
confectioners' sugar, for dusting

1 Tie a double strip of wax paper around a 6½-cup capacity soufflé dish to make a 3-inch collar. Brush the inside with melted butter.
2 Melt the chocolate with the 1 tbsp milk (see page 12). Remove from the heat.
3 Melt the butter in a large heavy-based saucepan. Add the flour and cook 1 minute, then remove from the heat and gradually blend in the remaining milk and the cinnamon. Bring to a boil, stirring all the time, and cook about 1 minute.
4 Cool slightly, then beat in the egg yolks, sugar, and melted chocolate.
5 Beat the egg whites until stiff but not dry. Beat one spoonful into the sauce mixture to lighten it, then carefully fold in the remaining egg whites.
6 Gently pour the soufflé mixture into the prepared dish and level the top. Stand the dish on a baking sheet.
7 Bake in a preheated 375°F oven until well risen, just set, and well browned, 35–40 minutes. Remove the paper and dust lightly with confectioners' sugar. Serve immediately.

POIRES BELLE HÉLÈNE

SERVES 6

⅔ cup sugar
thinly pared rind and juice of
2 oranges
6 firm pears
8 oz bittersweet chocolate
¼ cup orange-flavored liqueur
orange slices, for decoration

1 Put the sugar, 3¾ cups water, and half the orange rind in a large, heavy-based saucepan and heat gently, without stirring, until the sugar has dissolved.

2 Meanwhile, peel the pears quickly, leaving the stems on. Cut out the cores from the base and level the bases.

3 Stand the pears in the syrup, cover the pan, and simmer gently until tender, about 20 minutes. Let cool, covered, basting occasionally with the syrup.

4 Cut the remaining orange rind into thin matchstick (julienne) strips. Blanch in boiling water 2 minutes, then drain and immediately refresh under cold running water. Let drain on paper towels.

5 Melt the chocolate with the liqueur (see page 12) and let cool slightly.

6 Remove the pears from the syrup and stand them on a large serving dish or six individual dishes. Chill 2 hours.

7 Discard the orange rind from the syrup. Stir the melted chocolate into ⅔ cup of the syrup with the orange juice, then slowly bring to a boil, stirring constantly. Simmer, stirring, until the sauce is thick and syrupy.

8 To serve, pour the hot chocolate sauce over the cold pears and sprinkle with the orange julienne. Decorate with orange slices and serve immediately.

STEAMED CHOCOLATE PUDDING

Serve with vanilla ice cream or one of the sauces on page 153. Make the sauce while the pudding is steaming and reheat just before serving.

SERVES 4

2 oz bittersweet chocolate
1 tbsp unsweetened cocoa powder, sifted
6 tbsp milk
1⅓ cups fresh white bread crumbs
½ cup (1 stick) butter or margarine, softened
½ cup + 1 tbsp sugar
2 eggs
¾ cup self-rising flour

1 Half-fill a large saucepan or steamer with water and bring to a boil. Grease a 5-cup capacity pudding basin or steaming mold. Melt the chocolate (see page 12), then blend in the cocoa powder with 1 tbsp of the milk.

2 Put the breadcrumbs in a small bowl and pour over the remaining milk. Let them soak.

3 Meanwhile, cream the butter and sugar together until pale and fluffy. Beat in the eggs, flour, melted chocolate, and soaked bread crumbs. Spoon into the prepared basin and make a slight hollow in the center. Cover with greased wax paper and foil, and secure with string. Put the basin in the saucepan or steamer and cover with a tightly fitting lid. Steam until well risen and firm to the touch, about 2 hours, adding more boiling water to the pan as necessary.

4 Carefully loosen the pudding from the basin, unmold, and serve with your chosen sauce or ice cream.

CHOCOLATE-PECAN TART

SERVES 10

For the pastry
2 cups all-purpose flour
3 tbsp unsweetened cocoa powder
⅛ tsp salt
10 tbsp unsalted butter, diced
2 tbsp sugar

For the filling
2 cups pecan halves
3 eggs, beaten
1 cup light brown sugar, firmly packed
1 cup evaporated milk
1 tsp vanilla extract
4 tbsp unsalted butter, melted

1 To make the pastry, sift the flour, cocoa powder, and salt into a large bowl. Add the diced butter and cut it in or rub it in with your fingertips until the mixture resembles coarse crumbs. Stir in the sugar. Gradually mix in 2–3 tbsp cold water until the dough begins to hold together (it will still be quite crumbly).

2 Turn the dough onto a lightly floured surface and shape it into a ball. Roll it out and use it to line a lightly greased 11-inch fluted tart pan with a removable base. Prick the pastry case all over with a fork, then chill 1 hour.

3 Line the pastry case with foil and fill with baking beans. Bake in a preheated 375°F oven 10 minutes. Remove the foil and beans, return the pastry case to the oven, and bake 5 minutes longer. Remove from the oven and let cool. Reduce the oven temperature to 325°F.

4 To make the filling, chop the pecans, reserving ½ cup well-formed halves for the decoration. Put the chopped nuts in a bowl and add the remaining filling ingredients. Mix well and pour into the pastry case. Arrange the pecan halves over the filling. Bake until set in the center, about 1 hour. Serve warm or cold with ice cream or whipped cream.

MARBLED HAZELNUT AND LEMON PUDDING

SERVES 6

⅓ cup hazelnuts, skinned and
toasted
½ cup soft margarine
½ cup + 1 tbsp sugar
2 eggs, beaten
1 cup + 3 tbsp self-rising flour
2 tbsp milk
finely grated rind of 1 lemon
2 tbsp unsweetened cocoa powder

1 Half-fill a large saucepan or steamer with water and bring to a boil. Meanwhile, grease a 1-quart capacity fluted brioche or cake mold with a funnel, or a kugelhopf mold. Cover the top of the hole in the center with a piece of foil to prevent water seeping in during steaming.
2 Put the nuts in a food processor and process until very finely ground. Tip into a mixing bowl. Wipe out the food processor with a piece of paper towel to remove any remaining nuts. Put the margarine, sugar, eggs, flour, and milk in the food processor and process until smooth, 2–3 minutes.
3 Remove half of the mixture and fold it into the ground hazelnuts with the lemon rind. Add the cocoa to the mixture remaining in the food processor and process until evenly mixed, about 1 minute.
4 Fill the prepared mold with these mixtures, adding them in alternate spoonfuls to create a marbled effect. Level the surface, cover with greased wax paper and foil, and secure with string. Put the mold in the saucepan or steamer and cover with a tightly fitting lid. Steam until well risen and firm to the touch, about 1½ hours, adding more boiling water to the pan as necessary. Carefully loosen the edges of the pudding from the mold, turn out, and serve with custard or chocolate sauce.

MOCHA FUDGE PUDDING

During cooking, this pudding separates to give its own built-in sauce. It's also good served with chilled sour cream.

SERVES 8

1 cup (2 sticks) butter or margarine,
softened
1½ cups light brown sugar, firmly
packed
2 eggs, beaten
6 tbsp coffee essence
1 cup + 3 tbsp self-rising flour,
sifted
⅔ cup unsweetened cocoa powder
½ cup chopped walnuts
2½ cups milk

1 Cream together the butter and 1 cup of the sugar. Gradually beat in the eggs with the coffee essence. Fold in the flour and cocoa powder with the walnuts, adding a little of the milk to give a soft consistency that drops from the spoon.
2 Spoon into a 2½-quart capacity buttered ovenproof dish.
3 Blend together the remaining brown sugar and the milk, and pour evenly over the pudding mixture. Bake in a preheated 325°F oven until spongy to the touch, about 1 hour 40 minutes.

STEAMED CHOCOLATE SOUFFLÉ WITH CHOCOLATE SAUCE

SERVES 6

2 tbsp unsalted butter
3 tbsp all-purpose flour
⅔ cup milk
3 oz bittersweet chocolate,
finely chopped
2 tbsp sugar
6 tbsp heavy whipping cream
3 eggs, separated
confectioners' sugar, for dusting

For the chocolate sauce
4 oz bittersweet chocolate,
finely chopped
2 tbsp brandy
⅔ cup heavy whipping cream
⅔ cup milk
1 tbsp unsalted butter
2 tsp cornstarch

1 Grease a 6-inch diameter, 3-inch deep soufflé dish with butter, then coat evenly with a little sugar.

2 Melt the butter in a saucepan, then stir in the flour. Remove from the heat and gradually stir in the milk, then add the chocolate. Heat gently, stirring all the time, until the chocolate melts, then cook until thickened. Remove the sauce from the heat. Beat in half the sugar, then beat in the cream and the egg yolks.

3 Beat the egg whites until stiff, but not dry, then gradually beat in the remaining sugar, beating until shiny. Add about one-third of the egg whites to the chocolate mixture and fold in carefully to loosen the mixture, then very gently fold in the remaining egg whites.

4 Pour the soufflé mixture into the prepared dish. Place a rack or an up-turned saucer in a heavy-based saucepan, stand the soufflé dish on the rack. then add enough boiling water to come about one-third of the way up the side of the dish. Cover the pan with a tightly fitting lid, then steam the soufflé gently until it is well risen and set, about 45 minutes, adding more boiling water to the saucepan if necessary.

5 Meanwhile, to make the chocolate sauce, put the chocolate, brandy, cream, and most of the milk into a small saucepan. Heat gently, stirring until the chocolate melts, then stir in the butter.

6 Blend the cornstarch with the remaining milk to form a smooth paste, then stir it into the sauce. Cook over medium heat until the sauce thickens slightly. Keep the sauce warm until ready to serve.

7 When the soufflé is cooked, remove it from the heat and let the soufflé settle 5 minutes (it will sink slightly). Unmold the soufflé onto a warmed serving dish and dust with confectioners' sugar. Serve immediately, with the chocolate sauce poured around it, or serve the sauce separately in a warmed pitcher.

CHOCOLATE MERINGUE TART

When meringue is broiled, as it is in this recipe, it becomes delightfully soft and marshmallowy. If you want to make the tart in advance, let the chocolate filling cool with a piece of wax paper lying on its surface to prevent a skin from forming.

SERVES 8–10

1 baked 9-inch Plain-Pastry Tart Shell (see page 84)

For the filling
2 tbsp sugar
5 tbsp flour
⅓ cup unsweetened cocoa powder
⅛ tsp salt
2 cups milk
4 oz bittersweet chocolate, finely chopped
3 egg yolks
1 tsp vanilla extract

For the meringue
3 egg whites
¾ cup superfine sugar

1 To make the filling, put the sugar, flour, cocoa powder, salt, milk, and chocolate in a heavy-based saucepan and heat very gently, stirring all the time. When the chocolate has melted, increase the heat and cook until boiling and thickened, about 5 minutes, whisking constantly.

2 Beat the egg yolks with the vanilla, then gradually beat in about half of the chocolate sauce. Return the mixture to the saucepan and heat very gently until thickened further, 1–2 minutes. (Do not let this mixture boil or it will curdle.) Pour the chocolate mixture into the cold tart shell.

3 To make the meringue, beat the egg whites until stiff, then add half of the sugar. Continue beating until the mixture is smooth and glossy, then gradually fold in the remaining sugar.

4 Preheat the broiler. Pile the meringue on top of the chocolate mixture, making sure that it completely covers the filling and the pastry edge. Place the tart under the broiler, 3–4 inches from the heat, and cook the meringue until it is golden brown and set, 2–3 minutes. Serve immediately.

BLACK BREAD PUDDING

This unlikely combination of flavors makes an interesting bread pudding. It also works well with other tart fruits, such as red currants and cranberries.

SERVES 6

3 eggs, separated
½ cup + 1 tbsp sugar
½ tsp ground cinnamon
⅛ tsp salt
8 cups fresh dark rye or pumpernickel bread crumbs
4 oz semisweet chocolate, grated
12 oz black currants, stems removed
2 tbsp light brown sugar, firmly packed
confectioners' sugar for dusting

1 Grease an 8-inch diameter soufflé dish.

2 Beat the egg yolks, sugar, and cinnamon together until pale and fluffy.

3 Beat the egg whites with the salt until stiff, then fold into the egg yolk mixture with the bread crumbs and chocolate. Arrange the black currants in the prepared dish and sprinkle with the brown sugar. Pour the bread mixture over the fruit.

4 Bake in a preheateed 350°F oven until firm to the touch, about 40 minutes. Dust with confectioners' sugar and serve hot or cold with sour cream.

CHAPTER FOUR
COLD DESSERTS

RICH-PASTRY TART SHELL

MAKES ONE 9-INCH TART SHELL

1⅔ cups all-purpose flour
½ tsp salt
6 tbsp butter, chilled and diced
7 tbsp sugar
4 egg yolks
½ tsp vanilla extract

1 Sift the flour and salt onto a work surface. Make a well in the center and add the remaining ingredients.
2 Using the fingertips of one hand, pinch and work the sugar, butter, and egg yolks together until well blended.
3 Gradually work in all the flour to bind the mixture together. Knead lightly until smooth.
4 Wrap the dough in foil or plastic wrap and let it "rest" in the refrigerator or a cool place about 30 minutes.
5 Roll out the dough on a lightly floured surface and use to line a 9-inch fluted tart pan with a removable base. Prick the bottom of the shell. Cut out a piece of wax paper or foil larger than the pastry shell. Lay the paper or foil in the pastry shell and fill with baking beans to weigh it down.
6 Bake in a preheated 425°F oven 10 minutes, then reduce the oven temperature to 375°F and bake until lightly browned 5–10 minutes longer.
7 Cool slightly in the pan, then remove and cool on a wire rack.

PLAIN-PASTRY TART SHELL

MAKES ONE 9-INCH TART SHELL

½ cup + 1 tbsp butter, margarine, or
shortening
1⅔ cups flour
⅛ tsp salt

1 Cut the fat into the flour and salt until the mixture resembles fine crumbs. Add 3–4 tbsp chilled water and stir in with a round-bladed knife until the mixture comes together.
2 Knead lightly to make a firm, smooth dough, taking care not to over-handle the dough or the pastry will be tough.
3 Roll out the dough on a lightly floured surface and use to line a 9-inch fluted tart pan with a removable base. Cover with foil and "rest" in the refrigerator for 30 minutes before lining with paper or foil weighed down with baking beans and baking as for the Rich-Pastry Tart Shell (see left).

CHILLED ITALIAN CHEESECAKE

This cake is best made a day or two before serving and chilled overnight. If your food processor is small, you will have to blend the cheese filling and the crumb topping in two batches.

SERVES 10

⅔ cup shelled hazelnuts

4 oz bittersweet chocolate, roughly chopped

grated rind and juice of 1 lemon

1½ lb ricotta cheese

2 tbsp dark rum

¾ cup sugar

2 eggs + 1 egg white

14 tbsp cold butter

2⅓ cups all-purpose flour

2½ tsp baking powder

½ cup light brown sugar, firmly packed

¾ cup ground almonds

1 tsp vanilla extract

confectioners' sugar, for dusting

1 Grease a 9-inch springform cake pan and line the bottom with parchment paper.

2 Toast the hazelnuts under the broiler until browned, place in a dish towel, and rub off the skins. Let cool, then place in a food processor with the chocolate, lemon rind and lemon juice, the cheese, rum, and sugar. Process until just combined, then turn into a large bowl. Lightly beat the extra egg white until it just holds its shape and fold it into the mixture.

3 Cut the butter into 1-tbsp portions and place in the food processor with the flour, baking powder, brown sugar, almonds, vanilla, and eggs. Process until the mixture resembles coarse crumbs.

4 Spoon one-third of the crumb mixture into the bottom of the prepared cake pan and lightly press into place. Top with the ricotta mixture, leveling the surface, then spoon over the remaining crumb mixture and spread evenly. Make sure the surface is covered, but leave the top of the cheesecake quite rough.

5 Set the pan on a baking sheet and bake in a preheated 350°F oven until slightly risen, golden brown, and firm to the touch, about 1 hour. Let the cheesecake cool in the pan, then cover and refrigerate overnight.

6 Before serving, take the cake out of the refrigerator and remove it from the pan. Leave at room temperature about 1 hour before serving, dusted with confectioners' sugar.

CHOCOLATE ROULADE

Don't worry if the cake cracks as you roll it – the cracks are part of its charm.

SERVES 8–10

For the roulade
4 oz bittersweet chocolate
4 eggs, separated
½ cup + 1 tbsp sugar
2 tbsp unsweetened cocoa powder, sifted

For the filling
⅔ cup heavy whipping cream
1 tbsp confectioners' sugar
⅔ cup thick plain yogurt
a few drops of rose water (optional)
8 oz raspberries

For the sauce and decoration
1 lb raspberries
1 tbsp kirsch
confectioners' sugar
white chocolate curls (see page 13)
a few raspberry or mint leaves

1 Grease a 13-×9-inch shallow baking pan, line with parchment paper, and grease the paper.
2 To make the roulade, melt the chocolate (see page 12) and let it cool slightly.
3 Beat the egg yolks and sugar together in a bowl until very thick and pale. Beat in the chocolate. In a separate bowl, beat the egg whites until stiff, then fold carefully into the chocolate mixture with the cocoa powder. Pour the batter into the prepared pan and spread evenly.
4 Bake in a preheated 350°F oven until well risen and firm to the touch, about 20 minutes.
5 While the cake is baking, lay a piece of wax paper on a flat work surface and sprinkle generously with sugar. When the cake is cooked, unmold onto the paper. Carefully peel off the lining paper. Cover the cake with a clean, damp dish towel and let cool.
6 To make the filling, whip the cream with the confectioners' sugar until it forms soft peaks. Fold in the yogurt with a few drops of rose water, if using. Spread the cream over the cake. Sprinkle with the raspberries. Starting from one of the narrow ends, carefully roll up the cake, using the paper to help. Transfer the roulade to a serving plate and dust generously with confectioners' sugar.
7 To make the sauce, push the raspberries through a strainer, or purée in a blender or food processor, then strain to make a smooth, seedless purée. Add the liqueur and sweeten to taste with confectioners' sugar.
8 Serve the roulade decorated with confectioners' sugar, white chocolate curls, and raspberry or mint leaves, and accompanied by the raspberry sauce.

PROFITEROLES

Always assemble all the ingredients before starting to make choux pastry as it is important to add all the flour quickly as soon as the mixture has come to a boil. Raw choux paste is too soft and sticky to be rolled out and is, therefore, piped or spooned onto a dampened baking sheet for baking. During baking, the moisture in the dough turns to steam and puffs up the mixture, leaving the center hollow. Thorough cooking is important; if insufficiently cooked, the choux may collapse when taken from the oven and there will be uncooked dough in the center to scoop out.

SERVES 4

For the choux pastry
½ cup all-purpose flour
4 tbsp butter or margarine
2 eggs, lightly beaten

For the chocolate sauce
4 oz bittersweet chocolate
1 tbsp butter or margarine
2 tbsp light corn syrup
2–3 drops of vanilla extract

For the filling and decoration
¾ cup heavy whipping cream
confectioners' sugar, for dusting

1 To make the choux pastry, sift the flour onto a plate or piece of paper. Put the butter and ⅔ cup water in a saucepan. Heat gently until the butter has melted, then bring to a boil. Remove the pan from the heat and tip the flour all at once into the hot liquid. Beat thoroughly with a wooden spoon.

2 Continue beating the mixture over the heat until it is smooth and forms a ball in the center of the pan. (Take care not to overbeat or the mixture will become fatty.) Remove from the heat and let the mixture cool 1–2 minutes.

3 Beat in the eggs, a little at a time, adding only just enough to give a consistency suitable for piping. It is important to beat the mixture vigorously at this stage to trap in as much air as possible. A portable electric mixer is ideal for this purpose. Continue beating until the mixture develops an obvious sheen.

4 Spoon the choux pastry into a pastry bag fitted with a ½-inch plain tube. Pipe about 20 small bun shapes on two dampened baking sheets.

5 Bake in a preheated 425°F oven until well risen and golden brown, 20–25 minutes. Reduce the oven temperature to 350°F. Remove the puffs from the oven and make a hole in the side of each with a skewer or knife to release the steam. Return to the oven to dry out completely, about 5 minutes. Let cool on a wire rack.

6 To make the chocolate sauce, melt together the chocolate, butter, 2 tbsp water, the corn syrup, and vanilla in a small saucepan over very low heat. Stir well until smooth and well blended.

7 Whip the cream until it just holds its shape. Spoon into a pastry bag fitted with a medium plain tube and use to fill the choux puffs through the holes in the sides.

8 Dust the profiteroles with confectioners' sugar and serve with the chocolate sauce spooned over or served separately.

Variation
Chocolate Eclairs Make the choux paste as above, then pipe 2½-inch long strips on dampened baking sheets. Bake as above and cool on a wire rack. Fill with cream and dip the tops in melted chocolate or glacé icing made with 1 cup confectioners' sugar and 2 tsp unsweetened cocoa powder blended with a little hot water.

MOCHA REFRIGERATOR CAKE

This quick and easy dessert requires no cooking.

SERVES 6

3 tbsp brandy
1 cup freshly made strong black coffee
4 oz semisweet chocolate
½ cup confectioners' icing sugar
½ cup (1 stick) unsalted butter, softened
2 egg yolks
1¼ cups heavy whipping cream
½ cup chopped almonds, toasted
about 30 ladyfingers
candy coffee beans, for decoration

1 Grease an 8½-×4½-inch top measurement loaf pan and line the bottom with wax paper. Grease the paper. Stir the brandy into the coffee.

2 Melt the chocolate with 1 tbsp water (see page 12). Remove from the heat and let cool for about 5 minutes.

3 Sift the confectioners' sugar into a bowl. Add the butter and beat together until pale and fluffy. Add the egg yolks, beating well.

4 Lightly whip the cream and chill half of it. Stir the remaining cream, the cooled chocolate, and the nuts into the butter and egg yolk mixture.

5 Line the bottom of the prepared pan with ladyfingers, cutting to fit if necessary. Spoon over one-third of the coffee and brandy mixture.

6 Layer the chocolate mixture and remaining ladyfingers in the pan, soaking each layer of ladyfingers with coffee and ending with soaked ladyfingers. Weigh down lightly and chill until set, 3–4 hours.

7 Unmold, remove the paper, and decorate with whipped cream and coffee beans.

CHOCOLATE CUSTARD TART

SERVES 8

1 baked 9-inch Plain-Pastry Tart Shell (see page 84)

For the filling and decoration
½ cup +1 tbsp sugar
6½ tbsp all-purpose flour
⅛ tsp salt
2 cups milk
2 oz bittersweet chocolate
3 egg yolks
3 tbsp butter or margarine
1 tsp vanilla extract
1 cup heavy whipping cream
chocolate curls (see page 13) or grated chocolate, for decoration

1 To make the filling, mix the sugar, flour, and salt in a large saucepan and stir in the milk. Break the chocolate into small pieces and add it to the pan. Heat gently until the chocolate has melted, stirring constantly. Whisk until the chocolate and milk are blended, then increase the heat and cook about 10 minutes, stirring constantly. Remove the pan from the heat.

2 Beat the egg yolks and whisk in a small amount of the hot chocolate sauce. Slowly pour the egg mixture into the saucepan, stirring rapidly. Cook over low heat, stirring, until the mixture is very thick and creamy, 10–15 minutes. Do not let it boil. Remove from the heat.

3 Stir the butter and vanilla into the chocolate custard, then pour into the cold tart shell. Cover to prevent a skin from forming and chill until set, about 4 hours.

4 Just before serving, whip the cream lightly and spread evenly over the chocolate filling. Decorate the top with chocolate curls or grated chocolate. Serve chilled.

WHISKY-CHOCOLATE TART

This tart is made with a coffee-flavored bavarian mixture and topped with whisky cream. We made ours in a heart-shaped mold.

SERVES 6–8

3 oz bittersweet chocolate
1 baked 9-inch Rich-Pastry Tart
Shell (see page 84)

For the filling
2 tsp unflavored gelatin
⅔ cup milk
1 tbsp instant coffee granules
3 egg yolks
1 tbsp sugar
⅔ cup heavy whipping cream

For the topping
1 cup heavy whipping cream
1–2 tbsp Scotch whisky
1 tbsp sugar
chocolate caraque (see page 13), for
decoration

1 Melt the chocolate (see page 12). Place the tart shell, upside-down, on a sheet of wax paper. Using a pastry brush, brush half of the melted chocolate evenly all over the outside of the tart shell. Leave in a cool place until the chocolate sets. Turn the tart shell over and brush the inside with the remaining chocolate. Leave in a cool place to set.

2 To make the filling, sprinkle the gelatin over 2 tbsp water in a small heatproof bowl and let it soak 2–3 minutes. Place the bowl over a saucepan of simmering water and stir until the gelatin has dissolved.

3 Put the milk and coffee granules into a small saucepan. Heat gently until the coffee dissolves completely and the milk comes almost to a boil. Very lightly whisk the egg yolks and sugar together in a heatproof bowl. Pour in the coffee-flavored milk and mix well.

4 Place the bowl over a pan of hot water and cook the custard, stirring constantly, until it is thick enough to coat the back of the spoon. As soon as the custard thickens, strain it through a nylon strainer into a clean bowl. Stir in the dissolved gelatin. Let the custard cool, stirring frequently to prevent a skin from forming.

5 Whip the cream until it will just hold soft peaks, then gently fold it into the coffee custard. Place the chocolate-coated tart shell on a flat serving plate and fill it with the coffee cream mixture. Chill until set.

6 To make the topping, whip the cream with the whisky and sugar until it will just hold soft peaks. Spread an even layer of cream over the top of the tart. Whip the remaining cream until thick enough to pipe and fill a pastry bag fitted with a medium star tube. Pipe whirls of cream around the top of the tart, then decorate with chocolate caraque. Chill before serving.

CHOCOLATE MACAROON LOG

To make the hazelnut flavor more pronounced, substitute ground, unblanched hazelnuts for the almonds when making the macaroons, and omit the almond extract.

SERVES 10

For the macaroons
whites from 3 medium eggs
2 cups ground almonds
1½ cups superfine sugar
1½ tsp almond extract

For the filling and decoration
¾ cup shelled hazelnuts
4 oz bittersweet chocolate
1¼ cups heavy whipping cream
3 tbsp almond-flavored liqueur
confectioners' sugar, for dusting
unsweetened cocoa powder, for dusting
chocolate leaves (see page 15)
shelled hazelnuts

1 To make the macaroons, line two baking sheets with parchment paper. Beat the egg whites until stiff, then fold in the almonds, sugar, and almond extract.

2 Spoon the mixture into a pastry bag fitted with a ½-inch plain tube and pipe 30 small rounds on the prepared baking sheets, allowing room around them for the mixture to spread.

3 Bake in a preheated 350°F oven about 20 minutes. Transfer to a wire rack and let cool 20 minutes.

4 To make the filling, spread the nuts on a baking sheet and brown them in the oven at 400°F for 5–10 minutes. Tip onto a dish towel and rub off the skins. Chop finely.

5 Melt the chocolate (see page 12) and let it cool 5 minutes.

6 Whip the cream until it holds its shape. Gradually fold in the cooled chocolate, nuts, and liqueur.

7 Use some of the chocolate cream to put pairs of macaroons together. Place them side by side on a serving plate to form a double log. Spread chocolate cream on top and add a further layer of macaroons. Spread the remaining chocolate cream over the top and sides of the macaroon log. Chill overnight in the refrigerator.

8 To serve, dust with confectioners' sugar and cocoa powder, then decorate with chocolate leaves and whole hazelnuts.

CHOCOLATE, CHESTNUT, AND GINGER TART

SERVES 12

1 baked 9-inch Rich-Pastry Tart Shell (see page 84)

For the filling
*2 oz bittersweet chocolate
⅓ cup stem ginger syrup
(from the jar)
2 eggs
5 tbsp sugar
⅔ cup heavy whipping cream
15-oz can unsweetened chestnut purée
white and dark chocolate curls
(see page 15), for decoration*

1 To make the filling, melt the chocolate with the ginger syrup (see page 12) and remove from the heat.

2 Beat the eggs and sugar together until very pale and thick. Whip the cream until it holds its shape and fold in the cool but not cold chocolate. Fold into the egg mixture.

3 Whip the chestnut purée with one-quarter of the chocolate mixture until smooth. Gradually beat in the remaining mixture. Cover and chill at least 1 hour.

4 About 30 minutes before serving, spoon the mixture into the cold tart shell. Decorate with chocolate curls.

PETITS POTS DE CRÈME

If you do not have the special little china pots for making this rich cream, you can use small ramekin dishes. A less rich cream can be made by using milk instead of cream.

SERVES 6–8

*2½ cups light whipping cream
½ tsp vanilla extract
8 oz bittersweet chocolate, broken into small pieces
5 egg yolks + 1 whole egg
2 tbsp sugar*

1 Put the cream, vanilla, and chocolate into a saucepan and heat gently, stirring, until the chocolate melts and the mixture is smooth.

2 Lightly mix together the egg yolks, whole egg, and sugar, then stir in the chocolate cream. Strain the mixture through a nylon strainer into eight ⅓-cup petits pots, or six ½-cup ramekins. Cover the petits pots or ramekins with lids or small rounds of foil.

3 Set the dishes on a rack in a large, wide saucepan, and add enough boiling water to come about halfway up the sides of the dishes. Cover the pan with a lid, then steam the creams over very low heat until they are very lightly set and the centers are still slightly soft, about 15 minutes. Do not overcook or the smooth texture will be spoiled. Remove from the pan and let cool. Chill well before serving.

CHOCOLATE-CINNAMON TART

Two-tone chocolate leaves make a stunning decoration for this tart which, when sliced, reveals its layers of creamy chocolate and cinnamon custard.

SERVES 6–8

1 quantity piecrust
(see Plain-Pastry Tart Shell
page 84)

For the filling
1¼ cups milk
1 vanilla bean
1 tbsp unflavored gelatin
3 eggs, separated
½ cup + 1 tbsp sugar
2 oz semisweet or milk chocolate
1 tsp ground cinnamon

For the decoration
two-tone chocolate leaves
(see page 15)

1 Roll out the dough very thinly and use to line a deep 9½-inch fluted flan ring set on a baking sheet. Line with wax paper or foil and weigh down with baking beans. Bake in a preheated 400°F oven until golden brown and cooked through, 20–25 minutes. Remove the paper and baking beans and let cool.

2 To make the filling, put the milk and vanilla bean in a small saucepan and bring to a boil. Remove from the heat, cover, and let infuse about 30 minutes.

3 Sprinkle the gelatin over 3 tbsp water in a small heatproof bowl and let it soak 2–3 minutes. Place the bowl over a pan of simmering water and stir until dissolved.

4 Whisk the egg yolks and 7 tbsp of the sugar together in a bowl until very pale and thick. Remove the vanilla bean from the milk. Return the milk to a boil and pour onto the egg mixture, whisking constantly.

5 Return the mixture to the pan and heat gently, without boiling, until it thickens enough to coat the back of a wooden spoon. Remove from the heat, add the dissolved gelatin, and stir.

6 Divide the mixture between two bowls. Break the chocolate into one bowl and stir until melted. Cool until beginning to set. Whisk the cinnamon into the other bowl. Cool until beginning to set.

7 Beat the egg whites until stiff but not dry. Add the remaining sugar and beat again until stiff. Fold half the meringue mixture into each custard.

8 Pour half the chocolate custard into the tart shell. Freeze for a few minutes to set. Cover with the cinnamon custard and freeze quickly to set. Finish with the remaining chocolate mixture. Decorate with chocolate leaves and chill until ready to serve.

MAKING MOUSSES AND COLD SOUFFLÉS:
YOUR PROBLEMS SOLVED

● Separate the eggs carefully. Just a trace of yolk in the egg white will make it almost impossible to beat to any volume.

● Lightly whip the cream until it just holds its shape. Beat the egg white until it forms soft peaks so that it can be mixed evenly into the mousse or soufflé. The trick is to get all the mixtures to a similar consistency so that they fold together quickly and evenly. Over-beaten egg whites make a lumpy, unevenly textured mousse.

● Similarly, aim to have all your ingredients at the same temperature: Don't use cream straight from the refrigerator. If it is too cold, it will cause anything that's added to it (such as dissolved gelatin or melted chocolate) to set and harden.

● Dissolve soaked gelatin very gently; don't let the water boil furiously underneath the bowl. If the gelatin gets too hot and boils, it will not set the mixture.

● Always cool melted chocolate before adding it to a mousse or soufflé.

● Use a chocolate high in chocolate liquor for the most intense flavor.

● If the mixture begins to set before the egg white is added, don't panic. Set the bowl over a pan of gently simmering water until the warmth is sufficient to melt the mixture again. Don't let the mixture get too hot, and stir frequently, then let cool again and complete as directed. The finished mousse or soufflé won't be quite as light and airy as it could be, but it will be perfectly acceptable.

● The young, the elderly, pregnant women, and people with immune-deficiency diseases should not eat raw eggs due to the possible salmonella risk.

WHITE CHOCOLATE AND SHERRY MOUSSE

The chocolate horns can be made in advance. The filled horns will keep in the refrigerator up to 2 days. Pack them in a single layer in a rigid container. Serve with a refreshing red fruit salad.

SERVES 8

4 oz white chocolate
3 tbsp dry sherry wine or eau de vie
⅔ cup heavy whipping cream
2 eggs, separated
1 tsp unflavored gelatin
1 tbsp milk
16 chocolate horns (see page 18),
for serving (optional)
chocolate shapes (see page 16), for
decoration

1 Melt the chocolate with the sherry and 2 tbsp water (see page 12). Stir well until the mixture is smooth, then beat in the egg yolks.
2 Lightly whip the cream until it just holds its shape. Fold in the chocolate mixture.
3 Sprinkle the gelatin over the milk in a small heatproof bowl and let soak 2–3 minutes. Place the bowl over a pan of simmering water and stir until the gelatin has dissolved. Stir into the chocolate mixture. Chill until beginning to set.
4 Beat the egg whites until stiff but not dry, then fold into the chocolate mixture. Chill until set to the consistency of whipped cream.
5 Stand the chocolate horns in tall glasses or mugs and spoon in the mousse. Alternatively, spoon the mousse directly into individual serving dishes. Chill at least 1 hour before serving, decorated with chocolate shapes.

CHOCOLATE AND LIME MOUSSE

Lime adds a refreshing tang to the chocolate flavor of this mousse.

SERVES 2

3 oz bittersweet chocolate
2 eggs, separated
1 tbsp sugar
finely grated rind and strained juice
of 1 small lime
⅔ cup heavy whipping cream
½ tsp unflavored gelatin
grated chocolate or twists of lime,
for decoration

1 Melt the chocolate (see page 12) and let it cool slightly.
2 Beat the egg yolks with the sugar and lime rind until thick and mousse-like. Beat in the chocolate, then 2 tbsp of the cream.
3 Sprinkle the gelatin over the lime juice in a small heatproof bowl and let it soak 2–3 minutes. Place the bowl over a saucepan of simmering water and stir until the gelatin has dissolved. Beat into the chocolate mixture.
4 Beat the egg whites until stiff but not dry, then fold into the chocolate mixture.
5 Divide the mousse between two glasses and chill until set. Whip the remaining cream and use to decorate the desserts with grated chocolate or twists of lime. Leave at cool room temperature for about 30 minutes before serving.

CHOCOLATE MOUSSE CUPS

SERVES 6

*3 large sheets of phyllo pastry, each
measuring about 10 ×20 inches,
thawed if frozen
2 tbsp butter, melted
4 oz bittersweet chocolate
2 tbsp brandy
1 tbsp instant coffee powder
2 eggs, separated
⅔ cup heavy whipping cream
a few strawberries and
confectioners' sugar, for decoration
Stirred Egg Custard (see page 154)
and strawberry purée, for serving
(optional)*

1 Cut each phyllo pastry sheet into 12 squares. Line each cup of a 12-cup muffin tin with three overlapping squares, brushing with melted butter between each layer.
2 Bake in a preheated 400°F oven until the pastry is crisp, golden brown, and cooked through, 10–12 minutes. Unmold onto a wire rack and let cool.
3 Break the chocolate into small pieces and put it in a heatproof bowl with the brandy, coffee powder, and 1 tbsp water. Set the bowl over a pan of simmering water and heat gently until the chocolate melts. Stir the mixture until smooth.
4 Stir the egg yolks into the chocolate mixture and let it cool slightly. Lightly whip the cream and fold it into the chocolate mixture. Beat the egg whites until stiff but not dry, then fold into the chocolate mixture. Chill until set to the consistency of thick cream. Spoon the mousse into the pastry cups and chill 1 hour.
5 Decorate each cup with a few strawberries and dust heavily with confectioners' sugar before serving with custard sauce and a little strawberry purée, if desired.

CHOCOLATE AND ORANGE TRIFLE

Use purchased chocolate cake or use up home-made cake that's a little stale.

SERVES 8

*12 oz chocolate sponge cake
4 large, juicy oranges
½ cup orange-flavored liqueur
4 egg yolks
5 tbsp sugar
3 tbsp cornstarch
a few drops of vanilla extract
2½ cups milk
3 tbsp stem ginger syrup
(from the jar)
1¼ cups heavy whipping cream
toasted almonds and stem ginger,
for decoration*

1 Thinly slice the cake and use it to line the bottom of a shallow serving dish.
2 Peel and section the oranges. Arrange the sections on top of the cake. Spoon the liqueur evenly over the cake and oranges.
3 In a heavy-based, preferably non-stick, saucepan, combine the egg yolks, sugar, cornstarch, and vanilla. Gradually stir in the milk and ginger syrup. Bring the mixture almost to a boil and simmer until thickened, 4–5 minutes, stirring all the time.
4 Pour the custard evenly into the dish and let it cool.
5 Whip the cream until it just holds its shape, then spoon on top of the custard. Decorate with almonds and stem ginger.

Opposite: Chocolate Mousse Cups

DARK AND LIGHT CHOCOLATE TERRINE

A wickedly delicious chocoholic's dream! Be careful when slicing, as the terrine softens very quickly.

SERVES 6–8

For the praline
1⅔ cups blanched almonds or
skinned hazelnuts
½ cup + 1 tbsp sugar

For the dark chocolate mousse
6 oz bittersweet chocolate
6 tbsp unsalted butter, softened
7 tbsp sugar
2 tbsp unsweetened cocoa powder,
sifted
3 egg yolks
2 tbsp rum or brandy
1¼ cups heavy whipping cream

For the white chocolate mousse
6 oz white chocolate
4 tbsp unsalted butter, softened
2 egg yolks
⅞ cup heavy whipping cream

1 Grease a 3-cup capacity loaf pan and line it with plastic wrap. Lightly oil a baking sheet.

2 To make the praline, toast the nuts in a preheated 350°F oven until golden brown, stirring occasionally. Put the sugar in a heavy-based saucepan with 1 tbsp water. Heat gently until the sugar has dissolved, then stir in the warm nuts and boil until the syrup starts to brown. Immediately pour onto the prepared baking sheet. Let cool completely, then roughly crush with a rolling pin or in a blender or food processor. Store in an airtight tin until needed.

3 To make the mousses, melt both chocolates in separate bowls (see page 12). Stir until smooth, then let them cool slightly.

4 To make the dark chocolate mousse, cream the butter and half the sugar together until pale and creamy. Beat in the cocoa powder. In another bowl, beat the egg yolks and the remaining sugar together until pale. Stir in the rum. Whip the cream until it just holds its shape. Working quickly, beat the melted bittersweet chocolate into the creamed butter. Stir this into the yolk mixture, then carefully fold in the cream. Set aside.

5 To make the white chocolate mousse, beat the butter into the melted white chocolate. Stir in the egg yolks and 2 tbsp crushed praline. Whip the cream until it just holds its shape and fold into the chocolate mixture.

6 Drop large spoonfuls of each mousse alternately into the prepared pan until full. Tap the pan on the work surface to level the mixture. Cover and chill until very firm, at least 4 hours (preferably overnight).

7 To serve, unmold the mousse onto a flat serving dish and peel off the plastic wrap. With a metal spatula, press the remaining praline over the top and sides of the terrine. Chill 30 minutes to firm, then serve cut in slices. This dessert is so rich it needs nothing extra to accompany it.

CHOCOLATE-ORANGE SOUFFLÉ

SERVES 6–8

2 cups milk
5 oz bittersweet chocolate
3 eggs, separated + 1 egg white
7 tbsp sugar
1 tbsp unflavored gelatin
grated rind and juice of 1 orange
1¼ cups heavy whipping cream
1 tbsp chocolate-flavored liqueur
grated chocolate, for decoration

1 Tie a double strip of wax paper around a 1-quart capacity soufflé dish to make a 3-inch collar. Lightly brush the inside of the paper with oil.

2 Put the milk in a saucepan and add the chocolate. Heat gently until the chocolate melts, then bring almost to a boil.

3 Whisk the egg yolks and sugar together in a bowl until pale and thick. Gradually pour on the chocolate milk, stirring. Return to the pan and cook gently, without boiling, about 20 minutes, stirring, until the mixture coats the back of a wooden spoon.

4 Sprinkle the gelatin over 3 tbsp water in a small heatproof bowl and let soak 2–3 minutes. Place the bowl over simmering water and stir until the gelatin dissolves. Stir into the custard with the orange rind and juice. Let cool.

5 Whip the cream until it just holds its shape, then fold most of the cream into the cold mixture. Beat the egg whites until stiff, then fold into the mixture.

6 Pour the soufflé mixture into the prepared dish and chill until set. Carefully ease away the paper collar just before serving.

7 Stir the liqueur into the remaining cream and use to decorate the soufflé. Sprinkle the top with grated chocolate.

CHOCOLATE LACE BASKETS

These dainty lace baskets are made with compound chocolate coating. When set, it is less brittle than real chocolate and is therefore less likely to crack. Don't attempt these unless you have time to spare, as they require patience.

SERVES 6

5 oz semisweet compound chocolate coating
1 small mango
¼ fresh pineapple
12 strawberries
1 passion fruit
whipped cream, for serving

1 Melt the compound chocolate coating (see page 12).

2 Invert six 3½-inch ring molds and stretch plastic wrap over the rounded bases to cover completely.

3 Spoon half the melted chocolate covering into a parchment paper piping cone and snip off the point. Pipe three of the ring molds with a lacy pattern of chocolate covering.

4 Fill a second bag with melted chocolate covering and pipe the remaining three molds. Chill until set.

5 Meanwhile, peel the mango and chop the flesh, discarding the seed. Cut the pineapple flesh into pieces. Hull the strawberries. Halve the passion fruit and scoop out the pulp.

6 Carefully lift the chocolate baskets with the plastic wrap, then remove the wrap from the baskets. Fill the baskets with the fruit and serve with whipped cream.

CHOCOLATE- AND NUT-FILLED FIGS

Although this recipe uses figs that don't need soaking, as they're easier to fill, we still recommend soaking them.

SERVES 6

12 oz tenderized dried figs
6 tbsp orange-flavored liqueur, such
as Cointreau or Grand Marnier
⅔ cup water
¼ cup shelled unsalted pistachio
nuts
⅓ cup walnut halves
3 oz bittersweet chocolate, broken
into pieces
walnut halves, for decoration
(optional)
a mixture of plain yogurt and
cream, for serving

1 Place the figs in a bowl and pour over the liqueur and water. Cover and let soak about 3 hours.

2 Skin the pistachio nuts and put them in a food processor with the walnut halves and chocolate. Add 3 tbsp of the soaking juices and blend until roughly chopped.

3 Make a small hole in the stem end of each fig and use a teaspoon to fill with the stuffing. Close over the hole and top with a walnut half, if desired.

4 Place the figs, side by side, in an ovenproof dish and spoon over the remaining soaking juices. Serve cold with a mixture of yogurt and cream.

CARAMEL MOUSSE

This is a rich, easily made mousse, best left in the refrigerator overnight.

SERVES 6

three 61.5-g Mars bars
1 tbsp milk
1¼ cups heavy whipping cream
1 egg white

For the decoration
sugar
whipped cream
cape gooseberries

1 Thinly slice the Mars bars and put them in a heatproof bowl with the milk. Place over a saucepan of simmering water and heat gently, stirring occasionally, until melted and almost smooth. Let cool about 10 minutes, stirring occasionally.

2 Whip the cream until it just holds its shape, then gently stir a large spoonful into the Mars bar mixture. Fold in the remaining cream with a large metal spoon.

3 Lightly beat the egg white and fold it into the chocolate mixture. Pour into a bowl, cover, and let set in the refrigerator overnight.

4 To make crushed caramel for decoration, line a small baking sheet with foil and brush generously with oil. Sprinkle sugar evenly over the foil and cook under the broiler until melted and golden. (Don't take your eyes off it for a second as it can suddenly catch and burn.) As the sugar melts it will run into uneven pools of caramel. Remove from the broiler immediately and let cool slightly before peeling it off the foil and breaking into pieces. Use to decorate the mousse along with the whipped cream and cape gooseberries.

Opposite: Caramel Mousse

DOUBLE CHOCOLATE SOUFFLÉ

To serve this soufflé-in-a-case, use a warm knife to cut it into wedge-shaped pieces. It's very rich but irrestible! The finished, decorated soufflé can be frozen and simply thawed overnight when required.

SERVES 8

14 oz bittersweet chocolate
⅞ cup heavy whipping cream
2 tbsp brandy, rum, or Kahlua
2 tsp unflavored gelatin
3 eggs, separated
5 tbsp sugar
white, milk, and bittersweet
chocolate curls (see page 13), for
decoration
unsweetened cocoa powder, for
dusting

1 Lightly grease a deep 8½-inch cake pan with slightly sloping sides. Line the bottom and sides with parchment paper, keeping the sides as smooth as possible. Stand the pan on a baking sheet.

2 Melt half the chocolate (see page 12) and let it cool slightly.

3 Spoon the chocolate into the center of the pan. Gently tip and brush it up the sides of the pan to coat the bottom and sides evenly (a pastry brush will help). Freeze until firm, about 1 hour. Carefully ease off the pan and gently peel away the parchment paper. Place the chocolate case on a baking sheet in the refrigerator.

4 Melt the remaining chocolate with 3 tbsp of the cream and the brandy. Let the mixture cool slightly.

5 Sprinkle the gelatin over 2 tbsp water in a small heatproof bowl and let it soak 2–3 minutes. Place the bowl over a saucepan of simmering water and stir until the gelatin has dissolved.

6 Whisk the egg yolks with the sugar until thick and mousse-like. Stir in the dissolved gelatin and the cooled chocolate mixture. Lightly whip the remaining cream and fold it in.

7 Beat the egg whites until they form soft peaks and fold into the chocolate mixture. Pour gently into the chocolate case. Refrigerate until set, about 3 hours.

8 Decorate the soufflé with chocolate curls and leave at room temperature for 10–15 minutes to soften slightly before serving. Dust the top of the soufflé with cocoa powder to finish.

CHOCOLATE SNOWBALL

This luscious dessert must be left for at least 24 hours before eating. The outer layer forms a crust while the center remains soft and fudge-like.

SERVES 4–6

6 oz bittersweet chocolate
1½ tsp instant coffee granules
¾ cup sugar
¾ cup (1½ sticks) unsalted butter, diced
4 eggs
1 tbsp dark rum
1 cup heavy whipping cream
sugared flower petals, for decoration (optional)

1 Line a 3-cup pudding basin with foil.
2 Melt the chocolate in a large heatproof bowl (see page 12). Dissolve the coffee in 3 tbsp water and add it to the bowl with the sugar. Heat gently until the sugar dissolves, then remove from the heat.
3 Beat the chocolate mixture thoroughly. Slowly beat in the butter until evenly combined. Beat in the eggs, one at a time. Stir in the rum. Pour the mixture into the prepared pudding basin.
4 Bake in a preheated 350°F oven until risen and firm, but still slightly wobbly, like a soufflé, with a thick, cracked crust, about 1¼ hours.
5 Let cool at room temperature, then press down to level the surface. Cover and chill at least 24 hours.
6 Unmold the dessert onto a serving plate and peel off the foil. Whip the cream until it holds its shape. Spoon the cream into a pastry bag fitted with a star tube and pipe rosettes on the pudding until it is completely covered. Decorate with a sprinkling of sugared petals, if desired.

MISSISSIPPI MUD PIE

This is a simpler version of the Frozen Mississippi Mud Pie on page 116. Serve warm with Chocolate Fudge Sauce (see page 153) or ice cream, or cold with whipped cream.

SERVES 16

For the crumb crust
1⅔ cups crushed gingersnaps
1⅔ cups crushed graham crackers
½ cup (1 stick) butter, melted

For the filling
1 cup (2 sticks) butter or margarine
6 oz bittersweet chocolate, broken into pieces
½ cup light corn syrup
4 eggs, beaten
½ cup chopped pecans

1 Grease a 9-inch springform cake pan.
2 To make the crust, mix the cookie crumbs with the butter. Press onto the bottom and 1½ inches up the sides of the prepared pan. Chill while making the filling.
3 To make the filling, put the butter, chocolate, and syrup in a saucepan and heat very gently until melted, stirring all the time. Let cool, then beat in the eggs and pecans. Pour the mixture into the crumb crust.
4 Bake in a preheated 350°F oven until just firm to the touch but still soft in the center, about 1¼ hours. Serve warm or cold with chocolate sauce, ice cream, or whipped cream.

CHOCOLATE HEAVEN

There are numerous versions of this wickedly rich concoction. This is our favorite.

SERVES ABOUT 12

⅔ cup shelled hazelnuts
1 lb couverture or bittersweet
chocolate, chopped
¼ cup brandy or orange-flavored
liqueur, or liqueur of your choice
⅓ cup light corn syrup
2½ cups heavy whipping cream
unsweetened cocoa powder and
chocolate wattles (see page 20),
for decoration

1 Oil a 10-inch springform cake pan. Line the bottom with wax paper and oil the paper.
2 Brown the hazelnuts under the broiler, shaking the pan occasionally so that they brown on all sides. Tip into a clean dish towel and rub off the skins. Broil again until thoroughly toasted, being careful not to let them burn. Let cool, then put them in a food processor and chop them very finely. Sprin-kle the finely chopped nuts evenly on the bottom of the prepared pan.
3 Put the chocolate, liqueur, and corn syrup in a large bowl. Set the bowl over a pan of simmering water and stir until the chocolate has melted. Remove the bowl from the saucepan and let cool slightly.
4 Lightly whip the cream until it *just* holds its shape. (Do not over-whip or the texture of the finished dessert will be ruined.) Fold one-quarter of the cream into the chocolate mixture, then fold in the remainder. Carefully pour into the prepared pan on top of the nuts. Tap the pan on the work surface once or twice to release any air bubbles. Cover with plastic wrap, then chill in the refrigerator several hours, preferably over-night, or until set.
5 To serve, carefully loosen the dessert from the sides of the pan with a metal spat-ula, then release the sides of the pan. Lift out on to a plate so that the nuts are still underneath. Dredge thickly with cocoa pow-der and decorate with chocolate wattles before serving.

CHOCOLATE BAVARIAN

SERVES 8

bland oil, such as sunflower
3¾ cups milk, or milk and light
whipping cream mixed
1 vanilla bean, split, or a few drops
of vanilla extract
4 oz bittersweet chocolate, chopped
6 egg yolks
5 tbsp sugar
4 tsp unflavored gelatin
1¼ cups heavy whipping cream
mixture of summer fruits (such as
strawberries, red currants, and
blueberries) and sweet herbs (such
as mint, chervil, and dill),
for decoration

For the fruit purée
8 oz black currants, stems removed
8 oz raspberries
½ cup sugar

1 Lightly oil a 1½-quart ring mold or a deep 1½-quart capacity cake pan or glass dish. Turn the mold upside-down on a piece of paper towel to let any excess oil drain off.

2 Put the milk in a saucepan with the vanilla bean, if using, and the chocolate. Heat gently until the chocolate has melted, then remove from the heat. Cover and let infuse 30 minutes.

3 Meanwhile, beat the egg yolks with the sugar until thick and almost white. Strain the milk onto the egg and sugar mixture and stir well until evenly blended. Add the vanilla extract, if using.

4 Rinse the saucepan, then pour the custard mixture back into it and cook over a low heat, stirring all the time with a wooden spoon, until it thickens enough to coat the back of the spoon, 10–12 minutes. Do not let the mixture boil or it will curdle. Don't rush this stage or the velvety texture of the custard will be lost. Strain into a large bowl,

cover the surface with damp parchment paper, and let cool at room temperature.

5 Sprinkle the gelatin over ¼ cup water in a small heatproof bowl and let soak 2–3 minutes. Set the bowl over a pan of simmering water and stir until the gelatin has dissolved.

6 Remove the parchment paper from the cooled (but not cold) custard. Pour in the dissolved gelatin, stirring well. Place the bowl in a roasting pan of water and surround with ice to speed up the process of thickening/setting. Stir constantly until the custard begins to resemble lightly whipped cream, about 15 minutes. Remove from the ice.

7 Working quickly, whip the cream until *just* beginning to thicken, then lightly fold into the custard with a large metal spoon. The trick is to get the cream to the same consistency as the custard. If too thick, it won't fold in evenly and will form small lumps through the mixture. If it is too thin, the custard will not hold any air and may become rather solid.

8 Pour the custard into the prepared mold and chill until set, at least 4 hours. Make sure that the refrigerator shelf is level or the finished bavarian will be lop-sided. Allow 4½–5 hours for the bavarian to set if using a deep cake pan or glass dish.

9 Meanwhile, place the black currants and raspberries in a saucepan with the sugar and 1¼ cups water. Heat gently until the sugar dissolves, then bring to a boil. Cover and simmer until the fruits are very soft, about 10 minutes. Let cool, then purée the contents of the pan in a blender or food processor. Strain into a bowl. Cover and store in the refrigerator.

10 To turn out the bavarian, gently ease the edges of the custard away from the mold with a dampened finger. This breaks the airlock. Moisten a flat plate and place it upside-down over the mold. Invert the plate and mold and give a series of gentle shakes sideways and down until the bavarian loosens. Carefully ease off the mold and slide the bavarian into the center of the plate. Bring to room temperature about 30 minutes–1 hour before serving. Moisten some of the mixed fruit with one or two spoonfuls of fruit purée, then spoon into the center of the bavarian. Pour a little of the purée around the dessert and decorate with fruit and fresh herbs. Serve the remaining purée separately.

CRANBERRY CREAMS

SERVES 8

2⅔ cups fresh or frozen cranberries
½ cup + 1 tbsp sugar
2 tbsp port wine
4 tsp unflavored gelatin
3 tbsp lemon juice, strained, or kirsch
6 oz white chocolate
1¼ cups light whipping cream
6 egg yolks
1¼ cups heavy whipping cream
grated white chocolate or white chocolate leaves (see page 15), for decoration

1 Lightly oil eight ½-cup ramekin dishes or custard cups. Line the bottoms and sides of the dishes with parchment paper.

2 Put the cranberries in a small saucepan with 7 tbsp of the sugar, the port, and 1¼ cups water. Bring to a boil, cover, and simmer gently until the cranberries begin to soften, about 10 minutes. Drain the berries, reserving the liquid.

3 Sprinkle 1 tsp gelatin over ⅞ cup of the reserved cranberry liquid in a heatproof bowl. (Return the remainder of the liquid to the reserved berries.) Let soak 2–3 minutes. Place the bowl over a saucepan of simmering water and stir until the gelatin has dis-

solved. Let cool and thicken slightly. Spoon into the prepared ramekin dishes or custard cups and refrigerate until set.

4 Sprinkle the remaining gelatin over the lemon juice or kirsch in a heatproof bowl. Let it soak.

5 Melt the chocolate with the light cream (see page 12). Stir until smooth.

6 Lightly whisk the egg yolks with the remaining sugar. Pour in the chocolate mixture, whisking constantly. Return to the bowl and cook over the simmering water, stirring, until thick enough to coat the back of a wooden spoon.

7 Add the gelatin and stir until completely dissolved, then let cool. Lightly whip the heavy cream and fold into the mixture. Divide among the ramekin dishes and return to the refrigerator to set.

8 To unmold the cranberry creams, place an individual serving plate upside-down on top of each ramekin and invert. Remove the lining paper. Decorate the creams with the reserved cranberry mixture and grated white chocolate or white chocolate leaves.

ZUCCOTTO

SERVES 6

3 tbsp brandy
2 tbsp orange-flavored liqueur
2 tbsp cherry- or almond-flavored
liqueur
12 oz pound cake
5 oz bittersweet or semisweet
chocolate
2 cups heavy whipping cream
1 cup confectioners' sugar
½ cup chopped toasted almonds
½ cup chopped toasted hazelnuts
confectioners' sugar and
unsweetened cocoa powder, for
decoration

1 Line a 1½-quart pudding basin or round-bottomed bowl with damp cheesecloth. In a separate bowl, mix together the brandy and liqueurs and set aside.

2 Cut the pound cake into ½-inch slices. Sprinkle with the brandy and liqueurs. Line the basin with the moistened cake, reserving enough to cover the top.

3 Using a sharp knife, chop 3 ounces of the chocolate into small pieces and set aside. Whip the cream and confectioners' sugar together until stiff, then fold in the chopped chocolate and nuts.

4 Divide this mixture in half and spread one half over the cake lining in an even layer.

5 Melt the remaining chocolate (see page 12). Let cool slightly, then fold into the remaining cream mixture. Use this to fill the center of the basin.

6 Level the top of the Zuccotto and cover with remaining moistened cake. Trim the edges. Cover and chill at least 12 hours.

7 To serve, uncover the Zuccotto and invert a flat serving plate over the top of it. Turn upside-down, lift off the bowl, and carefully remove the cheesecloth. Serve cold, dusted with confectioners' sugar and cocoa powder.

ALMOND AND HONEY WAFERS

The chocolate is surprisingly easy to pipe. Don't worry if the lattices are rough and irregular; they look better that way!

SERVES 6

5 oz bittersweet chocolate
4 oz white Toblerone candy bar
⅓ cup heavy whipping cream
about ⅔ cup sour cream
confectioners' sugar, for dusting
cape gooseberries, for serving

1 Line baking sheets with parchment paper. Melt the bittersweet chocolate (see page 12) and let it cool slightly. Spoon half the chocolate at a time into a small paper piping cone fitted with a fine icing tube.

2 Pipe thin lines of chocolate to form about 12 rough lattice shapes about 3 inches in diameter. Refrigerate to set.

3 Meanwhile, break the Toblerone into a bowl and add the heavy cream. Place over a pan of gently simmering water until the chocolate melts, then stir well to combine. (The mixture will not be completely smooth as there are chopped almonds in Toblerone bars.) Let cool. Mix in the sour cream, cover, and refrigerate.

4 To serve, peel the lattices off the lining paper. Put pairs of lattices together carefully with the Toblerone mixture. Keep chilled until serving time. Dust lightly with confectioners' sugar and serve with cape gooseberries.

CHAPTER FIVE

FROZEN DESSERTS

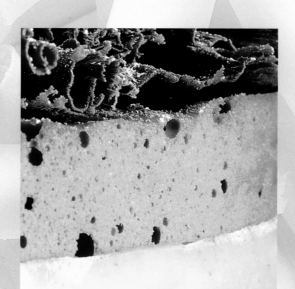

HOMEMADE ICE CREAM: YOUR PROBLEMS SOLVED

There is nothing to beat the rich flavor and creamy texture of homemade ice cream.

The knack of successfully achieving a smooth result largely depends on making sure that no large ice crystals form during freezing. This means that it is necessary to beat the freezing mixture periodically by hand if you are not using an ice cream machine, which will do the job for you.

Ice cream can be stored in the freezer up to 3 months.

To Freeze Ice Cream By Hand

The following freezing times, based on 1 quart ice cream, are given as a guide. If making a larger quantity of ice cream, the times should be increased.

1 If necessary, set the freezer to maximum or 'fast freeze' about 1 hour before you intend to freeze the mixture.

2 Make the ice cream mixture as directed.

3 Pour the mixture into a shallow, non-metallic freezer container. Cover and freeze until just frozen all over but still with a mushy consistency, about 3 hours.

4 Spoon into a bowl and mash with a fork or flat whisk to break down the ice crystals. Work quickly so that the ice cream does not melt completely.

5 Return the mixture to the shallow container and freeze again about 2 hours.

6 Mash again as described in step 4. If any other ingredients are to be added, such as nuts or chocolate chips, then fold them in at this stage.

7 Return to the freezer and freeze until firm, about 3 hours.

8 Remove from the freezer and let soften at room temperature 20–30 minutes before serving. (Do not forget to return the freezer setting to normal.)

Ice Cream Machines

An ice cream machine will freeze an ice cream mixture and churn it at the same time, thus eliminating the physical effort (unless it is a hand-cranked model). The results will be smooth and even-textured.

There are several types of ice cream machine available. Some use a mixture of ice and rock salt, some fit inside the freezing compartment of the refrigerator, and some have their own refrigeration unit.

Generally speaking, the cooled mixture should be poured into the machine when the dasher (paddle) is moving, otherwise it tends to freeze onto the bottom and sides of the bowl, stopping the dasher working. When making ice cream this way, if the recipe calls for whipped cream, it should be ignored. The cream can simply be added, unwhipped, with the custard.

Freezing time is usually about 20–30 minutes. The ice cream should then be transferred to the freezer and frozen 1–2 hours to let the flavors develop before serving. Soften slightly at room temperature before serving.

It is vital to clean ice cream machines thoroughly after using to prevent development of bacteria. Wash bowls, lids, dasher, and spatulas in the hottest water temperature possible. Be sure to wash and dry all parts that come into contact with salt to prevent corrosion.

DOUBLE CHOCOLATE ICE CREAM

SERVES 4–6

1 vanilla bean or ¼ tsp vanilla
extract
1¼ cups milk
4 oz bittersweet chocolate, broken
into pieces
3 egg yolks
5–7 tbsp sugar
1¼ cups heavy whipping cream
⅓ cup semisweet chocolate chips

1 Split the vanilla bean, if using, to reveal the seeds. Put the milk, vanilla bean, and bittersweet chocolate in a heavy-based saucepan and heat gently until the chocolate has melted. Increase the heat and bring almost to a boil. Remove from the heat, cover, and let infuse about 20 minutes.

2 Beat the egg yolks and sugar together in a bowl until well blended. Stir in the milk and strain back into the pan. Cook the custard over low heat, stirring all the time, until it thickens very slightly. It is very important not to let the custard boil or it will curdle. Pour into a bowl and let cool.

3 Whisk the cream into the cold custard mixture, with the vanilla extract, if using.

4 Freeze the mixture in an ice cream machine or by hand to the end of step 5 (see page 112). Mash again, then stir in the chocolate chips. Freeze until firm. Let soften at cool room temperature 20–30 minutes before serving.

BITTER CHOCOLATE AND LIQUEUR ICE CREAM

SERVES 4–6

1¼ cups milk
3 oz semisweet chocolate, broken
into pieces
1 oz unsweetened chocolate, broken
into pieces
2 tbsp orange-flavored liqueur
3 egg yolks
6–8 tbsp sugar
1¼ cups heavy whipping cream

1 Put the milk in a heavy-based saucepan and bring almost to a boil. Meanwhile, melt the chocolate with the liqueur (see page 12).

2 Beat the egg yolks and sugar together until well blended. Stir in the milk and strain back into the pan. Cook the custard over low heat, stirring all the time, until it thickens very slightly. It is very important not to let the custard boil or it will curdle. Remove the custard from the heat and stir in the melted chocolate until evenly blended, then pour into a bowl and let cool.

3 Whisk the cream into the cold custard mixture. Freeze the mixture by hand or in an ice cream machine (see page 112). Let soften at cool room temperature 20–30 minutes before serving.

CHOCOLATE FLAKE ICE CREAM

SERVES 4–6

1 vanilla bean or ¼ tsp vanilla
extract
1¼ cups milk
3 egg yolks
5–7 tbsp sugar
1¼ cups heavy whipping cream
2 chocolate bars, shaved into flakes

1 Split the vanilla bean, if using, to reveal the seeds. Put the milk and vanilla bean in a heavy-based saucepan and bring almost to a boil. Remove from the heat, cover, and let infuse about 20 minutes.

2 Beat the egg yolks and sugar together until well blended. Stir in the milk and strain back into the pan. Cook the custard over low heat, stirring all the time, until it thickens very slightly. It is very important not to let the custard boil or it will curdle. Pour into a bowl and let cool.

3 Whisk the cream into the cold custard mixture, with the vanilla extract, if using, and half of the flaked chocolate.

4 Freeze the mixture by hand or in an ice cream machine (see page 112), folding in the remaining flaked chocolate just before the ice cream is completely frozen. Let soften at cool room temperature for 20–30 minutes before serving.

FROZEN CHOCOLATE TERRINE WITH BRANDIED PRUNES

SERVES 14

8 oz tenderized pitted prunes
⅔ cup cold tea
3 tbsp brandy
8 oz bittersweet chocolate
4 eggs, separated
¾ cup confectioners' sugar, sifted
⅓ cup unsweetened cocoa powder,
sifted
1¼ cups heavy whipping cream

1 Put the prunes, tea, and brandy in a bowl and let soak 3–4 hours or overnight. Drain, reserving the liquid, then roughly chop the prunes.

2 Melt the chocolate (see page 12), then let it cool slightly.

3 Beat the egg whites and confectioners' sugar together to make a stiff meringue. Fold in the cocoa powder.

4 Whip the cream until it just holds soft peaks. Beat the egg yolks until pale and fluffy, then beat in the chocolate.

5 Carefully fold the egg yolk and chocolate mixture into the meringue, followed by the cream. Fold in the soaked prunes and the reserved liquid.

6 Pour the mixture into a 5-cup capacity terrine. Cover and freeze until firm, at least 5 hours.

7 To serve, dip the terrine briefly in hot water, then unmold it onto a serving plate. Serve cut in slices with light cream.

Opposite: Frozen Chocolate Terrine with Brandied Prunes; Chocolate Nut Snaps (page 140)

ICED BLACK FOREST CAKE

The cake quickly softens to give a delicious base for this dessert.

SERVES 8

2 eggs
7 tbsp sugar
6½ tbsp all-purpose flour
⅓ cup unsweetened cocoa powder, sifted

For the filling and decoration
16-oz can pitted cherries
2 tbsp kirsch
1 pint vanilla ice cream
½ cup toasted sliced almonds
chocolate curls (see page 13)

1 Grease an 8-inch round cake pan and line the bottom with wax paper. Dust with a little sugar and flour.
2 Beat the eggs and sugar together until pale and thick. Gently fold in the flour and cocoa powder, and spoon into the prepared pan.
3 Bake in a preheated 350°F oven until firm to the touch, about 30 minutes. Unmold onto a wire rack and let cool.
4 To make the filling, drain the cherries, reserving the juice. Mix 6 tbsp juice with the kirsch. Finely chop the cherries.
5 Cut the cake horizontally into two layers and place the base on a flat plate. Spoon on half the kirsch and juice, and all the cherries. Top with spoonfuls of ice cream, then add the second layer of cake and remaining juices. Sprinkle with sliced almonds and chocolate curls.
6 Place immediately in the freezer and freeze at least 3 hours. Overwrap once firm. Let soften at cool room temperature about 40 minutes before serving, cut in wedges.

FROZEN MISSISSIPPI MUD PIE

The origin of Mississippi Mud Pie is rather vague; our research led us to some unusual recipes and unlikely tales. According to one story, the recipe originated on the banks of the Mississippi, where the coffee-colored clay was baked into small edible pies — hence the name. Many recipes use ice cream to make the pie. We tried our version in the freezer and discovered it tasted wonderful, so we recommend serving it as a frozen dessert.

SERVES 16

For the crumb crust
4 tbsp butter
1 cup crushed graham cruackers
1 cup crushed gingersnaps

For the filling
2½ cups heavy whipping cream
2¼ cups sugar
¼ cup cornstarch
4 eggs
½ cup (1 stick) butter, diced
1 tsp vanilla extract
2 tbsp rum
2 tsp chicory and coffee essence

For the topping and decoration
4 oz bittersweet chocolate
2 eggs, separated
⅔ cup heavy whipping cream
confectioners' sugar and
unsweetened powder, for dusting
chocolate curls (see page 13)

1 Lightly oil an 8-inch springform cake pan and line the bottom and sides with parchment paper.
2 To make the crumb crust, melt the butter, then let it cool slightly. Add the cookie crumbs to the butter and stir until evenly combined. Press the crumb mixture evenly over the bottom of the prepared pan. Chill

until firm, about 30 minutes.

3 To make the filling, put the cream and sugar in a heavy-based non-stick saucepan and heat very gently, stirring occasionally, until the sugar has completely dissolved. Remove from the heat. Mix the cornstarch to a smooth paste with ¼ cup cold water. Lightly beat the eggs.

4 Stir the cornstarch and beaten eggs into the cream and sugar mixture and beat well until thoroughly combined and smooth. Return the mixture to the heat and slowly bring to a boil, stirring constantly with a wooden spoon, until the mixture becomes very thick and smooth, like fudge. This will take 15–20 minutes.

5 Beat the butter into the fudge mixture, one piece at a time, with all the remaining filling ingredients, until well combined and the mixture is very smooth and creamy once more.

6 Pour the filling over the chilled crumb base. Let it cool completely, then freeze at least 1 hour, preferably overnight, to set.

7 For the topping, melt the chocolate (see page 12). Whisk the egg yolks and cream together until well blended.

8 Add the cream mixture to the melted chocolate and whisk until smooth. Place in a small, heavy-based saucepan over low heat and stir constantly until the mixture is smooth and thickly coats the back of a wooden spoon, about 10 minutes. Do not boil or the mixture will curdle. Remove from the heat and let cool completely. Press a damp piece of parchment paper gently onto the surface to prevent a skin from forming.

9 When the chocolate mixture is cool, lightly beat the egg whites until they just hold soft peaks. Stir about one-third into the chocolate mixture, then gently fold in the remainder.

10 Pour the chocolate mixture evenly over the set fudge filling, leveling the surface if necessary with a round-bladed knife. Return to the freezer and freeze at least 2–3 hours or overnight, until solid.

11 To serve, remove the set pie from the pan. Gently peel off the lining paper and dust lightly with confectioners' sugar and cocoa powder. Sprinkle with the chocolate curls. Let soften at room temperature for 10–15 minutes before cutting.

Note

If you don't want to use the whole pie at once, it can be cut into serving portions at the end of step 9.

Overleaf: Frozen Mississippi Mud Pie

CASSATA

This Neapolitan specialty is traditionally served at Easter or other festivities, such as weddings. In its native country it is shaped in a special metal container called a *stampo da spumante*, which is dome-shaped with a lid, similar to our "bombe" mold. We found it just as easy to layer the ice cream in a pudding basin and the results were just as stunning. Cassata needs a lot of on-off attention, so start making it early in the day.

SERVES **8**

For the ice cream
3 egg yolks
7 tbsp sugar
1¼ cups milk
2 oz bittersweet chocolate
8 oz ripe strawberries, hulled and sliced
¼ tsp vanilla extract
⅔ cup heavy whipping cream

For the center filling
3 tbsp shelled unsalted pistachio nuts
⅔ cup heavy whipping cream
1 egg white
5 tbsp sugar
grated rind of 1 lemon

For the sauce
12 oz ripe strawberries, hulled
3 tbsp confectioners' sugar
1–2 tbsp Cointreau

1 To make the basic ice cream mixture, whisk the egg yolks and sugar together until pale and thick. Heat the milk until it almost reaches boiling point, and pour onto the egg mixture, whisking well. Strain back into the pan and cook over low heat, stirring all the time, until the custard thickens slightly, 10–12 minutes. Do not boil. Strain into a bowl and let cool.

2 Melt the chocolate with 1 tbsp milk (see page 12). Stir gently until smooth. Meanwhile, purée the 8 ounces of strawberries in a blender or food processor, then push through a nylon strainer to extract most of the seeds. Add two-thirds of the cool custard to the chocolate, stirring to blend. Stir the remaining custard and the vanilla extract into the strawberry purée.

3 Lightly whip the cream until it just begins to hold its shape. Stir two-thirds into the cold chocolate mixture and the remainder into the strawberry purée. Pour into separate shallow freezer containers, cover, and freeze by hand (see page 112).

4 Place a disk of parchment paper in the bottom of a 5-cup pudding basin. Place the empty basin in the freezer. Let the chocolate ice cream soften at room temperature for about 20 minutes. Line the basin evenly with chocolate ice cream, using a metal spoon. Freeze until firm, about 1½ hours.

5 Take the strawberry ice cream out of the freezer and let it soften at room temperature 20–30 minutes. Again working with a spoon to make it more pliable (it will be firmer than the chocolate ice cream), use to make a second lining of ice cream in the basin. Cover and freeze until firm.

6 Pour boiling water over the pistachio nuts, let stand 10 minutes, and then skin and roughly chop. Whip the cream until it just holds its shape. Beat the egg white until stiff but not dry. Beat in the sugar until smooth, then fold in the cream with the nuts and grated lemon rind.

7 Spoon the mixture into the center of the ice cream layers and level the top. Cover and freeze until firm, 4–4½ hours.

8 Meanwhile, to prepare the sauce, slice the strawberries. Purée the berries with the confectioners' sugar and Cointreau in a blender or food processor. Press the purée through a nylon strainer to remove the small seeds. Chill well before serving with the cassata.

9 To remove the cassata from the mold, let soften in the refrigerator 10 minutes. Immerse the sides of the pudding basin in lukewarm water about 15 seconds. Gently loosen the top edges of the ice cream, invert onto a serving plate, and shake gently. Carefully lift off the mold and discard the paper disk. Return to the freezer to firm up the outside if necessary. Cut in wedges to serve.

INDIVIDUAL COFFEE BOMBES WITH TRUFFLE CENTERS

These delicious bombes with a surprise center will not fail to impress. Replace the Chocolate Flake Ice Cream with any of the others in this chapter, if preferred.

SERVES 6

1½ quantities Chocolate Flake Ice Cream (see page 114)

For the filling
⅔ cup cake crumbs
⅓ cup ground almonds
2 oz bittersweet chocolate
3 tbsp heavy whipping cream
2 tbsp rum or brandy
chocolate leaves (see page 15) or caraque (see page 13), for decoration

1 If necessary, set the freezer to fast-freeze. Put six ¾-cup capacity individual freezer-proof tart or dessert molds, or ramekin dishes, in the freezer to chill.

2 Let the ice cream soften at room temperature until soft enough to spread, 20–30 minutes.

3 Meanwhile, to make the truffle filling, mix the cake crumbs and almonds together in a bowl. Melt the chocolate with the cream (see page 12). Add the chocolate mixture to the crumb and almond mixture with the rum. Mix well.

4 Spread the softened ice cream over the bottom and sides of the molds or dishes, leaving a cavity in the center for the truffle mixture. Freeze until firm, about 1 hour.

5 Fill the center of each mold with the truffle mixture and level the surface. Cover and freeze until firm, about 1 hour.

6 To serve, dip the molds or dishes briefly in hot water, then unmold onto serving plates. Return to the freezer for 10 minutes to firm up. Decorate and serve.

FROZEN CHOCOLATE, RUM, AND RAISIN CAKE

SERVES 12

For the filling
⅓ cup raisins
¼ cup dark rum
5 tbsp sugar
3 egg yolks
6 oz bittersweet chocolate
1¼ cups heavy whipping cream

For the crumb crust
6 tbsp butter or margarine, melted
2⅔ cups crushed chocolate-covered graham crackers

1 Put the raisins and rum in a small bowl and let soak several hours or overnight.

2 To make the crumb crust, mix the butter and cracker crumbs together. Press over the bottom of an 8-inch springform cake pan. Chill 30 minutes or overnight.

3 To make the filling, put the sugar and 5 tbsp water in a small saucepan and heat gently until the sugar has dissolved. Increase the heat and boil the mixture rapidly 4 minutes to make a syrup.

4 Meanwhile, drain the raisins, reserving any excess rum. Lightly whisk the egg yolks with the reserved rum. Gradually pour the sugar syrup onto the egg yolks, whisking all the time.

5 Melt the chocolate (see page 12). Stir into the egg yolk mixture and let cool.

6 Whip the cream until stiff, then fold into the cold chocolate mixture. Fold in the raisins. Pour the mixture into the pan on top of the crumb base.

7 Cover tightly with plastic wrap and foil, then freeze until firm, at least 3–4 hours. Remove from the freezer 5 minutes before serving, cut in wedges.

CHOCOLATE SORBET

This is delicious served with a little Kahlua or Tia Maria poured over.

SERVES 4

½ cup + 1 tbsp sugar
⅓ cup unsweetened cocoa powder
½ tsp instant coffee powder
1 egg white

1 Put the sugar, cocoa powder, and 1¼ cups water in a heavy-based saucepan. Heat gently until the sugar dissolves, then bring to a boil and boil rapidly 2 minutes, without stirring. Remove from the heat, add the coffee powder, and stir until dissolved. Let cool completely.

2 Pour the mixture into a shallow freezer container, cover, and freeze until mushy, about 3 hours.

3 Beat the egg white until stiff. Turn the sorbet into a bowl and beat gently to break down the ice crystals. Fold in the egg white. Return to the freezer container, cover, and freeze until firm, about 4 hours.

4 Transfer the sorbet to the refrigerator about 10 minutes before serving to let it soften slightly.

CHAPTER SIX

CONFECTIONERY

DIPPED AND COATED CHOCOLATES: YOUR PROBLEMS SOLVED

● For a smooth, shiny, professional finish, there is no doubt that tempered couverture chocolate (see page 21) really does give the best result when making dipped chocolates. It is very viscous after tempering, making dipping easy. The chocolate sets to give a fine, crisp coating and it will not develop "bloom" during storage. The taste of a thin coating of really good bittersweet chocolate is far superior to any of the alternatives and well worth the effort of tempering. It is extremely difficult to apply a thin, even coating of ordinary chocolate (by "ordinary," we mean the kind bought for baking or eating in supermarkets) because it is not fluid enough, so we do not recommend you use this for dipping chocolates.

● If you intend to make a lot of chocolate-coated confectionery, it is worth investing in a proper dipping fork or ring. This makes dipping easier, because a dipping fork has a long, straight handle and long, thin tines. After dipping, the fork can be used to create a professional decoration (see right).

● A wide, fairly shallow bowl is best for dipping; a very deep bowl makes the action of lifting out the chocolates awkward.

● To achieve the perfect coating, a certain amount of practice and technique is required. Fully immerse the chosen chocolate center in the melted chocolate, turn it around so that it is fully coated on all sides, then lift it up out of the chocolate by placing the fork tines or ring underneath it. Do not spear it. Lightly tap the neck of the fork on the edge of the bowl so that any excess chocolate runs back into the bowl.

Repeat this action a couple of times until the chocolate stops dripping, then draw the fork back across the bowl rim so that any excess chocolate that has collected on the base of the chocolate is wiped off. Carefully flip the chocolate over onto a piece of wax paper so that what was the top becomes the underside. (This gives a neater result than if you try to slide the chocolate off the fork – and it is easier than it sounds.) Decorate as desired (see below) before the chocolate sets. If your dipping has been successful, the finished chocolate will be without a pool, or "foot" (as it is known in the trade), of chocolate at the base. Let it set at room temperature. If you've used tempered chocolate, it will set very quickly.

● To give a professional finish, decorate the tops of the candies by touching them with the tines of a dipping fork or with a dipping ring. Do this immediately the chocolate has been dipped. Touch the surface with the fork or ring, then gently lift it up slightly (so that it is still in contact with the chocolate coating but not pressing on the center) and glide it across the surface. Your technique will improve with practice; once you've done this a few times, it becomes easy and very satisfying.

● Resist touching the chocolates while they are setting, or the smooth glossy surface will be ruined. The chocolate coating will be shinier if it is left to cool at room temperature (and if tempered chocolate or a very good quality chocolate has been used). In very hot weather, it may be necessary to refrigerate the chocolate to help it to set.

FRESH CREAM TRUFFLES

Coat just a few truffles at a time and put them in the refrigerator immediately. If you try to coat the whole batch, the first ones may start to melt.

MAKES ABOUT 45

⅔ cup heavy whipping cream
1 vanilla bean
1 egg yolk
2 tbsp sugar
5 oz bittersweet chocolate, broken into pieces
2 tbsp unsalted butter, softened

For the decoration
5 oz couverture chocolate or one of the alternatives (see page 22)
3 oz good-quality white chocolate
50 g (2 oz) white compound chocolate covering

1 Place the cream and vanilla bean in a small saucepan. Bring to a boil, then cover, and remove from the heat. Let the mixture infuse 20 minutes. Remove the vanilla bean.
2 Whisk the egg yolk with the sugar until very pale and thick. Whisk into the cream and return to the heat. Heat gently, without boiling, until it is beginning to thicken, 2–3 minutes, stirring all the time. Remove from the heat.
3 Add the bittersweet chocolate and stir until completely melted. Refrigerate the mixture until firm, about 1 hour.
4 Using an electric mixer, beat the softened butter into the chocolate and cream mixture.
5 Spoon the mixture into a pastry bag fitted with a ½-inch plain tube and pipe 1-inch lengths on a flat plate or baking sheet. Freeze until the cream has set completely, about 1 hour.
6 To decorate, temper the couverture chocolate (see page 21) or melt one of the alternatives (see page 12). Melt the white chocolate with the compound chocolate coating.
7 Coat half of the truffles with the dark chocolate and half with the white chocolate (see page 124 for detailed instructions on dipping). Pipe or drizzle white chocolate over the dark-chocolate-covered truffles and dark-chocolate over the white-chocolate-covered truffles. Refrigerate until set. Store in the refrigerator until required.

Overleaf: Fresh Cream Truffles

QUICK AND EASY TRUFFLES

Truffles based on cake crumbs are easier to handle than the classic chocolate and cream mixture (see Fresh Cream Truffles, page 125).

MAKES ABOUT 24

4 oz bittersweet chocolate
4 tbsp unsalted butter
2⅔ cups white or yellow cake crumbs
½ cup confectioners' sugar
1½ tbsp dark rum, brandy, or liqueur of your choice
⅔ cup unsweetened cocoa powder, confectioners' sugar, or chocolate sprinkles

1 Melt the chocolate with the butter (see page 12). Stir in the cake crumbs, confectioners' sugar, and spirit or liqueur of your choice. Cover and refrigerate until the mixture is firm enough to handle, about 30 minutes.

2 Lightly dust your fingers with confectioners' sugar and roll the truffle mixture into 24 small balls, then roll each one in the cocoa powder, confectioners' sugar, or chocolate sprinkles to coat completely.

3 Arrange the truffles in bonbon cases, then chill in the refrigerator until required. Remove from the refrigerator about 30 minutes before serving.

CHOCOLATE NUT TRUFFLES

Crumbs from a plain sponge cake are best for this recipe.

MAKES ABOUT 30

¾ cup shelled hazelnuts
4 oz bittersweet chocolate
6 tbsp butter, diced
3⅓ cups cake crumbs
2 tbsp confectioners' sugar
about 2 tbsp rum or brandy
unsweetened cocoa powder, for coating

1 Toast the nuts under the broiler until brown. Tip into a clean dish towel and rub off the skins. When cold, grind in a nut mill or food processor.

2 Melt the chocolate (see page 12). Let cool slightly, then stir in the butter until evenly blended. Add the nuts with the cake crumbs, confectioners' sugar, and rum or brandy to taste.

3 Chill the mixture in the refrigerator until firm, then roll into small balls and place on a baking sheet lined with wax paper.

4 Refrigerate, covered, until firm, then coat lightly in cocoa powder and return to the refrigerator until required. These truffles soften quickly at room temperature.

BITTER ORANGE CHOCOLATES

MAKES ABOUT 24

5 oz couverture chocolate or one of
the alternatives (see page 22)
finely grated rind and juice of
1 orange
1 tsp sugar
8 oz white chocolate
6 tbsp heavy whipping cream
2 tbsp unsalted butter
chopped almonds and confectioners'
sugar, for decoration (optional)

1 Temper the couverture chocolate (see page 21) or melt one of the alternatives (see page 12). Brush half the chocolate over the insides of 24 paper bonbon cases. Chill until firm. Use the remaining melted chocolate to brush on a second coat. Chill until firm.
2 Strain 3 tbsp orange juice into a saucepan, add the sugar, and heat gently until the sugar has dissolved. Bring to a boil and boil rapidly to reduce to 2 tbsp, 3–4 minutes. Let cool.
3 Melt the white chocolate with the cream (see page 12). Remove from the heat and whisk in the orange syrup and grated orange rind. Gradually beat in the butter. Cool until the mixture is the consistency of whipped cream, then pipe or spoon into the cases. Sprinkle with the almonds and dust with confectioners' sugar, if using. Cover loosely and store in the refrigerator.

Variation

Liqueur Chocolates Replace the orange syrup with 2 tbsp liqueur, such as Cointreau or Drambuie.

CINNAMON MERINGUE HEARTS

Small meringues are ideal as petit fours. Alternatively, pipe larger shapes about 2 inches long and serve as a dessert with a little cream to accompany.

MAKES ABOUT 70

2 egg whites
1/2 cup + 1 tbsp superfine sugar
1/2 tsp ground cinnamon, sifted
1 tbsp unsweetened cocoa powder,
sifted

For the filling and decoration
2/3 cup heavy whipping cream
4 oz bittersweet chocolate
unsweetened cocoa powder and
confectioners' sugar

1 Line two baking sheets with parchment paper.
2 Beat the egg whites until stiff but not dry. Beat in half the sugar until the mixture is stiff and shiny. Carefully fold in the remaining sugar with the cinnamon and cocoa powder.
3 Spoon the meringue into a pastry bag fitted with a small, plain 1/4-inch tube and pipe small heart shapes about 1 inch long on the lined baking sheets.
4 Bake in a preheated 275°F oven until completely dried out, about 1 hour. Remove with a metal spatula and transfer to a wire rack to cool. Store in an airtight container if not using immediately.
5 To make the filling, put the cream in a saucepan and bring to a boil. Meanwhile, chop the chocolate. Pour the cream over the chocolate, leave 5 minutes, then whisk until thoroughly mixed. Chill until firm.
6 About 1 hour before serving, put pairs of meringues together with the filling.
7 Dust with cocoa powder and confectioners' sugar. Refrigerate up to 2 hours.

SOLID CHOCOLATE EGGS

Ensure that the egg shells are thoroughly washed and dried before adding the chocolate.

MAKES 4

4 eggs
1 lb couverture chocolate, tempered
(see page 21), or bittersweet,
semisweet, milk, or white chocolate

For the decoration
crystallized violets
crystallized rose petals
melted chocolate

1 If you have never blown an egg before, now is the time to try. With a needle, pierce a tiny hole in each end of one of the eggs and blow out the contents. Enlarge the hole in one end to take a small piping tube and wash out the shell with cold water. Let dry thoroughly while you blow the rest of the eggs. (The warmth of a radiator will help with this.) When they are dry, put a piece of tape over the small hole in each egg so that it cannot leak.
2 Melt the chocolate (see page 12), if necessary. (If using tempered couverture chocolate, it will already be melted.)
3 Spoon the melted chocolate into a nylon pastry bag fitted with a small tube and pipe into the egg shells through the large holes. Swirl it around from time to time to remove any air bubbles. Let the eggs set overnight.
4 Carefully crack the eggs and peel off the shells. Decorate the solid chocolate eggs with crystallized violets, rose petals, and narrow ribbons, sticking them on with melted chocolate. Alternatively, wrap each egg tightly in colored foil. Place them in egg cups or arrange in a basket.

Variation
Marbled Eggs To make solid marbled Easter eggs, fill plastic egg molds with alternate spoonfuls of melted dark and white chocolate. Tap on the work surface to remove any air bubbles, then let set. Unmold the egg halves and stick together with a little melted chocolate.

CHOCOLATE EASTER EGG

Add liqueur to the truffles sparingly, or they'll turn out too soft. You may need to firm up the mixture in the refrigerator between shapings, anyway. The truffle recipe will fill two eggs; don't be tempted to use half quantity, or it will be difficult to work.

MAKES ONE 6-INCH EGG

10–11½ oz couverture chocolate, tempered (see page 21), or bittersweet, semisweet, milk, or white chocolate

For the truffles
*8 oz bittersweet or milk chocolate
6 tbsp heavy whipping cream
a few drops of brandy, rum, orange-flavored liqueur, coffee flavoring, or vanilla extract, to taste
chopped nuts, dried shredded coconut, chocolate sprinkles, or grated chocolate, for coating*

To assemble
*melted chocolate
ribbons
flowers (optional)*

1 Using cotton wool, polish the insides of two 6-inch plastic Easter egg molds. Place on a tray lined with parchment paper.
2 Melt the chocolate (see page 12), if necessary. (If using tempered chocolate it will already be melted.) Remove from the heat and let cool slightly.
3 Using a large spoon, pour enough melted chocolate into each mold in turn to coat the sides. Tilt the molds to coat completely.
4 Pour the excess chocolate back into the bowl. Invert the molds onto the parchment paper and refrigerate briefly until set. Apply a second coat of chocolate and refrigerate again. Repeat once more, then return to the refrigerator and leave 1 hour or until set. (If using tempered chocolate, aim to do these three coats before the chocolate sets in the bowl, or it will have to be re-tempered. If not using tempered chocolate, it can be re-melted if necessary.) The eggs will crack if removed from the refrigerator too soon.
5 To unmold the chocolate egg halves, trim any excess chocolate from the outer edge of the molds. Carefully pull each mold away from the chocolate around the edge to let air get in between the chocolate and the mold. Press firmly and the chocolate should slip out. Cover loosely and refrigerate.
6 To make the truffles, grate the chocolate into a small saucepan and add the cream. Heat gently until the chocolate has melted. Stir well and remove from the heat. Let cool to room temperature.
7 The mixture should have thickened considerably. Beat in the desired flavoring, then, preferably using an electric mixer, beat until the mixture is light and stands in peaks, about 5 minutes. Cover and refrigerate until quite firm.
8 Sprinkle a tray with your desired coating. Place teaspoonfuls of truffle mixture on a cool work surface. Dust your hands with cocoa powder or confectioners' sugar and quickly roll the mixture into balls. Roll the truffles in the coating and place on a baking sheet lined with parchment paper. Cover and refrigerate. The truffles will keep 4 days in the refrigerator.
9 To assemble the Easter egg, put the truffles in paper bonbon cases or Cellophane wrapping. Fill one half of the Easter egg with some of the truffles. Spread a little melted chocolate over the rims of the egg and, holding the remaining half in parchment paper, press it onto the melted chocolate to complete the egg. Refrigerate to set. Tie ribbons around the middle and decorate with flowers, if desired.

CHOCOLATE-COATED PECANS

Make sure the nut mixture is well chilled before coating and the chocolate will set quickly.

MAKES ABOUT 35

about 2 cups pecan halves
¼ cup confectioners' sugar
2 oz bittersweet, semisweet, or milk
chocolate, chopped
1 tbsp unsalted butter
6 oz couverture chocolate or one of
the alternatives (see page 22)

1 Put ½ cup of the nuts, the sugar, the chopped chocolate, and the butter in a food processor. Process until smooth.
2 Roll the mixture into small walnut-sized balls. Sandwich between two pecan halves and chill until firm.
3 Temper the couverture chocolate (see page 21) or melt one of the alternatives (see page 12). Dip the nuts into the chocolate to coat completely (see page 124 for detailed instructions on dipping). Let set on wax paper. Store in a single layer in an airtight container.

CHOCOLATE WALNUT CREAMS

The soft, smooth, nutty paste provides a delightful contrast in texture to the walnut halves. The distinctive shape of the walnut under the chocolate means that no final decoration is needed.

MAKES ABOUT 50

2½–3 cups walnut halves
½ cup + 1 tbsp sugar
1 tbsp orange juice
7 oz couverture chocolate or one of
the alternatives (see page 22)

1 Grind 1 heaped cup of the walnuts in a mill or food processor. Mix the ground nuts and sugar in a bowl, then add the orange juice and mix together to form a light paste. Knead the paste with your fingers until firm.
2 Roll out the walnut paste to about ¼-inch thickness on a board lightly dusted with confectioners' sugar. Cut into circles, using a 1-inch plain round cutter. Press a walnut half firmly into each round of paste.
3 Temper the chocolate (see page 21) or melt one of the alternatives (see page 12).
4 Dip the walnut rounds one at a time into the chocolate to give them a generous coating (see page 124 for detailed instructions on dipping). Place on wax paper to dry.

FILLED MOLDED CHOCOLATES

These are made in special molds which are available from specialty candymaking shops. It is difficult to give exact quantities since the molds vary, but the basic method is always the same.

Chocolate molds come in a variety of shapes and sizes. Some come as plastic or rubber sheets of molds, while individual metal or plastic shapes are also available. Depending on their size, they may be coated with a thin layer of chocolate and filled with ganache (see page 152), marzipan, or fondant; see below for the method. Alternatively, some have two halves (like an Easter egg mold) and may be used to make hollow shapes. Larger molds used to make hollow chocolate shapes will require at least two coats of chocolate for strength. Tempered couverture chocolate (see page 21) is easiest to handle and gives a professional, glossy finish that will last and not bloom. Ordinary melted chocolate can be used with satisfactory results for large molds, such as Easter eggs (see page 132). For alternatives to tempered couverture, see page 22.

It is quicker and easier to make filled chocolates in molds than to make individually dipped chocolates. Before you start, ensure that the molds are perfectly clean and dry, then polish them to a real shine with cotton wool. (The more you polish, the shinier the chocolate will be.) Use a small ladle to fill the indentations with tempered couverture chocolate or one of the alternatives (see page 22). Tap the mold sharply on the work surface to remove any air bubbles. Leave a few minutes to settle, then invert over the bowl of melted chocolate and let most of it run out of the molds, leaving a thin coating behind. Run a clean metal spatula across the top to scrape off any excess, then let set.

Once set, add the filling of your choice, filling the molds almost to the top. If using ganache, it's easiest to pipe it in with a pastry bag. If using fondant or marzipan, roll it into small balls and press gently into the chocolate-lined indentations. Pour over more chocolate to seal in the filling. Tap the mold on the work surface to remove any air bubbles and scrape off excess chocolate with a metal spatula. Let set, then unmold.

WHITE CHOCOLATE COLETTES

MAKES ABOUT 16

2 oz good-quality white chocolate
2 oz white compound chocolate
coating

For the filling and decoration
2 oz good-quality white chocolate
2 tbsp butter
2 tsp brandy
¼ cup heavy whipping cream
crystallized violets

1 Arrange 16 doubled bonbon cases on a baking sheet. Melt the chocolate and compound chocolate coating together (see page 12). Spoon a little into each paper case and use a brush to spread it to coat the inside of each case completely. Chill until set. Remelt the chocolate and repeat the process to make a thick chocolate shell.

2 To make the filling, melt the chocolate with the butter and brandy. Remove from the heat and leave about 10 minutes or until cool but not set.

3 Meanwhile, carefully peel away the paper from the chocolate cases. Whisk the cream into the cooled chocolate mixture and leave until thick enough to pipe. Spoon into a pastry bag fitted with a small star tube and pipe into the chocolate cases. Decorate with crystallized violets. Chill the colettes in the refrigerator at least 1 hour before serving.

QUICK CHOCOLATE AND NUT FUDGE

No fiddling with thermometers required for this melt-in-the-mouth fudge that only takes a few minutes to prepare. If you have a microwave oven, you can make it even quicker by melting the chocolate and butter with the milk on HIGH for 2–3 minutes. If using hazelnuts or macadamia nuts, the finished result will be improved if you toast the nuts before adding them to the fudge.

MAKES ABOUT 1 LB

½ cup (1 stick) butter, diced
3 oz bittersweet chocolate, chopped
¼ cup milk or cream
¼ cup unsweetened cocoa powder
3½ cups confectioners' sugar
1 cup roughly chopped Brazil nuts,
hazelnuts, or macadamia nuts

1 Grease a shallow 7-inch square pan and line with wax paper.

2 Put the butter, chocolate, and milk or cream in a large heatproof bowl. Set the bowl over a saucepan of simmering water and stir until the chocolate has melted.

3 Meanwhile, sift the cocoa powder with the confectioners' sugar. As soon as the chocolate has melted, tip the sugar mixture into the bowl and beat together until smooth. Beat in three-quarters of the nuts. Pour into the prepared pan, then tap vigorously on the work surface to level the surface of the fudge. Sprinkle the remaining nuts on top and press down lightly. Chill in the refrigerator until set, then cut into small squares. This fudge has a soft set, so it is best kept in the refrigerator.

CHOCOLATE FUDGE

MAKES ABOUT 1¾ LB

2¼ cups sugar
⅔ cup milk
10 tbsp butter
5 oz bittersweet chocolate, broken
into pieces
2½ tbsp honey

1 Lightly oil a shallow 7-inch square pan.
2 Heat all the ingredients gently in a large heavy-based saucepan, stirring until the sugar has dissolved.
3 Bring to a boil without stirring, then continue boiling until a temperature of 240°F is reached, stirring occasionally to prevent sticking. (Check the temperature on a candy thermometer.)
4 Remove the pan from the heat and set it on a cool surface to cool 5 minutes, then beat the mixture until thick, creamy, and beginning to "grain."
5 Pour into the prepared pan, mark into squares when almost set, and cut when cold.

CHOCOLATE ALMOND CRUNCH

The crunchy praline chocolate centers make a good contrast to the smooth chocolate coating. Crystallized violets make pretty decorations, but if you prefer to keep to nuts, top each chocolate with a slice of toasted almond.

MAKES ABOUT 25 PIECES

⅔ cup whole unblanched almonds
7 tbsp sugar
7 oz bittersweet chocolate
4 oz good-quality white chocolate
3 oz white compound chocolate
coating
crystallized violets or toasted sliced
almonds, for decoration

1 Oil a baking sheet. Put the almonds and sugar in a small, heavy-based saucepan and heat very gently until the sugar has dissolved, stirring to prevent the sugar sticking to the pan. Continue to heat until the sugar caramelizes to a light golden color and the nuts are lightly toasted.
2 Pour the mixture onto the prepared baking sheet and let set. When completely hard, finely crush the praline with a rolling pin or grind in a mill or food processor.
3 Melt the bittersweet chocolate (see page 12). Mix in the praline to make a stiff paste and turn it into a 7-inch square pan. Let it set.
4 Cut the chocolate praline into squares. Melt the white chocolate and compound chocolate coating (see page 12). Dip the chocolate praline, one piece at a time, into the chocolate to give a generous coating (see page 124 for detailed instructions on dipping). Before the coating dries, decorate each square with a piece of crystallized violet. Let set on wax paper.

HONEY AND CHOCOLATE FUDGE

The honey used in this recipe not only gives the fudge flavor, but stops it crystallizing as well, making it deliciously soft and creamy textured.

MAKES ABOUT 1½ LB

2¼ cups sugar
3 tbsp honey
2 cups canned sweetened condensed milk
½ cup (1 stick) butter
4 oz bittersweet chocolate, chopped
a few drops of vanilla extract

1 Oil a 7-inch square pan. Put the sugar, honey, condensed milk, and butter in a large, heavy-based saucepan and heat gently until the butter has melted and the sugar has completely dissolved, stirring constantly. Bring to a boil and boil to 240°F, stirring occasionally. (Check the temperature on a candy thermometer.)
2 Remove the pan from the heat and beat in the chocolate and vanilla a little, then beat until the mixture is thick enough to leave a trail when the beaters are lifted.
3 Pour the fudge into the prepared pan and let cool. Mark into squares as it begins to set. When completely cold and set, turn the fudge out and cut into the marked squares.

RUM AND RAISIN CUPS

There is a superb surprise filling of cake and raisins soaked in rum when you bite into these chocolates. They make a perfect Christmas gift.

MAKES ABOUT 40

5 oz couverture chocolate
5 oz bittersweet-flavour compound chocolate coating
2⅓ cups sponge cake crumbs
½ cup raisins
½ cup rum

1 Melt together the couverture and compound chocolate coating (see page 12). Using foil or doubled paper bonbon cases as molds, spoon a little chocolate into each case and use a small brush to coat the inside of each case completely. Leave to dry upside-down on parchment paper. Repeat, making about 40 chocolate cups. Apply a second coat of chocolate if the first one looks thin. Let set.
2 Mix the cake with the raisins. Cover with rum and let soak until all the rum is absorbed, about 30 minutes.
3 Spoon a little of the soaked cake and raisin mixture into the chocolate cups. Remelt the chocolate. Flood the tops of the cups, covering the filling completely to the edges. Let set.
4 When the tops are thoroughly dry, peel off the cases and place the chocolate cups in fresh cases.

CHAPTER SEVEN

COOKIES
AND
BARS

CHOCOLATE NUT SNAPS

(Photograph on page 115)
If you don't have time to make a paper piping cone, drizzle the chocolate decoration onto the cookies from a teaspoon.

MAKES ABOUT 2 DOZEN

1 egg, separated
½ cup + 1 tbsp sugar
3 oz bittersweet chocolate, finely chopped
1 cup toasted, skinned, and finely chopped hazelnuts
6½ tbsp all-purpose flour
⅔ cup ground almonds

For the decoration
2 oz dark or white chocolate
confectioners' sugar, for dusting

1 Grease two baking sheets. Beat the egg white until stiff, then stir in the remaining ingredients (including the egg yolk). Work the mixture with your fingers until it forms a ball of dough.

2 Turn the dough onto a lightly floured surface, knead lightly, and roll out until it is about ¼-inch thick. Using a 2-inch round cutter, cut out about 24 cookies, re-kneading and re-rolling the trimmings as necessary. Arrange the cookies on the prepared baking sheets.

3 Bake in a preheated 375°F oven until crisp, 12–15 minutes. Immediately ease the cookies off the baking sheets, put them on a wire rack, and let them cool.

4 To decorate the cookies, melt the chocolate (see page 12) and let it cool slightly. Lightly dust the cookies with confectioners' sugar. Make a parchment paper piping cone and spoon in the melted chocolate. Snip off the tip of the bag and pipe lines of chocolate across the cookies. Let set.

CHOCOLATE AND GINGER THINS

MAKES ABOUT 20

½ cup (1 stick) butter or margarine
1 cup + 3 tbsp all-purpose flour
5 tbsp sugar
1 oz bittersweet chocolate, finely chopped
3 tbsp finely chopped preserved stem ginger

For the icing
1 cup confectioners' sugar
2 tsp unsweetened cocoa powder
1 tbsp butter

1 Cut the butter into the flour and stir in the sugar, chocolate, and ginger. Knead together with your fingers until the mixture sticks together.

2 Turn the dough onto a lightly floured surface and roll it out thinly. Using a 2½-inch fluted round cutter, cut out about 20 cookies, re-kneading and re-rolling the trimmings as necessary. Arrange on greased baking sheets and bake in a preheated 375°F oven until just golden brown, 12–15 minutes. Transfer to a wire rack and let cool.

3 To make the icing, sift the confectioners' sugar and cocoa powder into a bowl. Add the butter and 2 tbsp hot water and blend until smooth. Dip half of each cookie in the icing, then let set on a wire rack.

ORANGE AND CHOCOLATE LOGS

These little logs are delicious plain or dipped in chocolate.

MAKES ABOUT 5 DOZEN

1 cup (2 sticks) + 2 tbsp butter or margarine, softened
½ cup confectioners' sugar
finely grated rind and juice of 1 orange
1⅔ cups all-purpose flour
¾ cup cornstarch
3 oz bittersweet chocolate

1 Cream the butter and sugar together until pale and fluffy. Beat in the orange rind and 2 tbsp strained orange juice.

2 Sift in the flours and mix until thoroughly smooth. Spoon the mixture into a pastry bag fitted with a ½-inch star tube.

3 Pipe the mixture onto greased baking sheets, making about 60 small logs 1½–2 inches long.

4 Bake in a preheated 350°F oven until sandy brown and just firm to the touch, about 15 minutes. Transfer to a wire rack and let cool.

5 Melt the chocolate (see page 12) and let it cool slightly. Dip in each log to half-coat in chocolate, then let dry on a wire rack.

FLORENTINES

For more elaborate florentines, to serve as petit fours, make them slightly smaller than here. Coat half with dark and half with milk chocolate, then pipe with contrasting lines of chocolate to decorate.

MAKES ABOUT 2½ DOZEN

7 tbsp butter
½ cup + 1 tbsp sugar
1⅓ cups sliced almonds, roughly chopped
3 tbsp golden raisins
5 candied cherries, chopped
3 tbsp chopped mixed candied peel
1 tbsp cream or milk
10 oz bittersweet chocolate

1 Line four baking sheets with parchment paper. Melt the butter in a saucepan over low heat, add the sugar, and boil the mixture 1 minute.

2 Remove the pan from the heat and add all the remaining ingredients, except the chocolate, stirring well to mix.

3 Drop the mixture in small heaps onto the prepared baking sheets, leaving space between each for the mixture to spread.

4 Bake in a preheated 350°F oven until golden brown, 10–15 minutes.

5 Remove from the oven and press around the edges of the cookies with the blade of a knife to neaten the shape. Leave on the baking sheets 5 minutes or until beginning to firm, then cool on a wire rack.

6 When the cookies are cool, melt the chocolate (see page 12) and let it cool until it coats the back of a spoon and is just beginning to set, 10–15 minutes.

7 Spread the chocolate over the backs of the cookies. Mark wavy lines in the chocolate with a fork and let set.

Overleaf: Florentines

CHOCOLATE AND HONEY FUDGE FINGERS

Divide this into small fingers as it's quite rich to eat. It's easy to make double the quantity and then keep a supply in the refrigerator; it will soon disappear!

MAKES ABOUT 12

8 oz graham crackers or any plain
cookies
⅔ cup raisins
2 oz semisweet chocolate
2 tbsp honey
6 tbsp butter or margarine

1 Oil a 7-inch square pan and line the bottom with wax paper.
2 Roughly crumble the crackers or cookies and add the raisins. Melt the chocolate, honey, and butter together in a small saucepan and stir into the crumbs.
3 Mix thoroughly and press firmly into the prepared pan.
4 Freeze 10 minutes or chill until firm, then cut into fingers. Store in the refrigerator until required.

CHOCOLATE CHIP AND MACADAMIA COOKIES

For petit-fours-sized cookies, roll the mixture into tiny balls, flatten, and bake about 7 minutes.

MAKES ABOUT 4 DOZEN

6 tbsp butter or margarine, softened
7 tbsp sugar
6 tbsp light brown sugar, firmly
packed
1 tsp vanilla extract
1 egg, beaten
1 cup + 3 tbsp self-rising flour
⅛ tsp salt
⅔ cup semisweet chocolate chips
¾ cup roughly chopped
macadamia nuts

1 Cream the butter until very soft. Gradually beat in the sugars and vanilla until evenly blended. Add the beaten egg and mix well.
2 Sift the flour and salt into the bowl. Fold carefully into the creamed butter and sugar mixture.
3 Add the chocolate chips and ½ cup of the macadamia nuts. Stir together to mix thoroughly.
4 Roll the mixture into balls about the size of marbles. Place on greased baking sheets, leaving space for spreading, and flatten lightly with a wet fork. Sprinkle the remaining chopped macadamia nuts on top of the cookies, pressing them down lightly.
5 Bake in a preheated 350°F oven until pale golden in color, about 10 minutes. Let cool slightly on wire racks. These are best eaten warm.

ALMOND-CHOCOLATE COOKIES

MAKES ABOUT 4 DOZEN

1 cup + 6 tbsp self-rising flour
⅔ cup sugar
¼ tsp freshly grated nutmeg
10 tbsp butter or margarine
1⅓ cups ground almonds
2 oz semisweet, sweet, milk or white,
chocolate, coarsely grated
1 egg, beaten
¼ tsp almond extract

1 Grease two or three baking sheets.
2 Put the flour, sugar, and nutmeg in a bowl. Cut the butter into the flour mixture until it resembles fine crumbs. Stir in the almonds and 1 ounce chocolate. Bind together with the egg and almond extract, then knead until smooth.
3 On a lightly floured surface, divide the dough in half and roll each half into a 12-inch long thin sausage shape. Wrap in wax paper or parchment paper.
4 Chill in the refrigerator until firm, about 30 minutes. Cut the rolls into slices about ½-inch thick and place well apart on the baking sheets. Flatten them lightly with the back of your hand. Bake in rotation in a preheated 375°F oven 15–20 minutes.
5 Let the cookies cool until just warm, then sprinkle the remaining chocolate over. Transfer to a wire rack and let cool completely.

CHOCOLATE OATIES

MAKES ABOUT 3½ DOZEN

¾ cup (1½ sticks) butter or
margarine, softened
1 cup light brown sugar, firmly
packed
2 oz semisweet chocolate
⅛ tsp salt
½ tsp baking powder
1 cup + 3 tbsp all-purpose flour
2¾ cups rolled oats
2 tbsp milk
½ tsp vanilla extract

1 Cream the butter and sugar together until pale and fluffy. Meanwhile, melt the chocolate (see page 12) and let it cool slightly.
2 Sift the salt, baking powder, and flour into the creamed mixture and add half of the oats and all the remaining ingredients (including the chocolate). Mix well and shape the mixture into walnut-sized balls. Roll the balls in the remaining oats until coated on all sides.
3 Spread out the balls on lightly greased baking sheets and bake in a preheated 350°F oven 25–30 minutes. Transfer to a wire rack and let cool.

MILLIONAIRES' SHORTBREAD

A wicked mixture of shortbread and caramel with a stunning marbled chocolate top. After sampling this, plain shortbread will never seem the same again!

MAKES ABOUT 12 SMALL SQUARES

½ cup + 2 tbsp all-purpose flour
2 tbsp sugar
4 tbsp butter

For the caramel and topping
4 tbsp butter or margarine
¼ cup light brown sugar, firmly packed
14-oz can condensed milk
3 oz semisweet chocolate
3 oz milk chocolate
3 oz white chocolate

1 To make the shortbread, mix the flour and sugar together in a bowl. Cut in the butter until the mixture resembles fine crumbs. Knead together until the mixture forms a ball, then press evenly into the bottom of a 7-inch square pan.

2 Bake in a preheated 350°F oven until firm to the touch and very lightly browned, about 20 minutes. Let cool in the pan.

3 To make the caramel, put the butter, sugar, and condensed milk in a saucepan and heat gently until the sugar has dissolved. Bring to a boil, stirring all the time, then reduce the heat and simmer very gently until the mixture has thickened and is a creamy fudge color, about 5 minutes. Pour over the shortbread and let cool.

4 When the caramel layer has cooled and set, melt the three different types of chocolate in separate bowls (see page 12). Place teaspoonfuls of the chocolate over the caramel, alternating the three types. Tap the pan on the work surface so that the different chocolates merge with each other, then use a skewer to create a marbled pattern. Chill until set, then cut into very small squares (it is very rich).

CHOCOLATE VIENNESE FINGERS

MAKES ABOUT 1½ DOZEN

*½ cup (1 stick) butter or margarine,
softened*
¼ cup confectioners' sugar
1 oz bittersweet chocolate
¾ cup all-purpose flour
¼ tsp baking powder
*1 tbsp sweetened cocoa powder
(instant cocoa)*
a few drops of vanilla extract
*2 oz semisweet, milk, or white
chocolate, for decoration*

1 Grease two baking sheets. Put the butter in a bowl and beat until pale and soft, then beat in the confectioners' sugar.
2 Melt the chocolate (see page 12) and let it cool 10 minutes. When the chocolate is cool, but not thick, beat it into the creamed mixture.
3 Sift in the flour, baking powder, and cocoa. Beat well, adding a few drops of vanilla extract.
4 Spoon into a pastry bag fitted with a medium star tube and pipe finger shapes about 3 inches long on the prepared baking sheets, leaving space between each for the mixture to spread. Bake in a preheated 375°F oven until crisp and pale golden, 15–20 minutes. Transfer to a wire rack and let cool 30 minutes.
5 When the cookies are cold, melt the chocolate for the decoration and dip both ends of the fingers into it. Leave on a wire rack until set.

Variation

Plain Viennese Fingers Omit the instant cocoa from the recipe above and add an extra 1 tbsp all-purpose flour.

TUILES

These cookies have to be curled up the moment they come out of the oven so don't try to bake too many at once. If they're left to cool down, they'll refuse to roll. They don't contain any chocolate but make a delicious accompaniment to chocolate desserts, such as the Caramel Mousse on page 102.

MAKES ABOUT 2 DOZEN

2 egg whites
*½ cup + 1 tbsp confectioners' sugar,
sifted*
½ cup all-purpose flour
5 tbsp butter, melted and cooled
confectioners' sugar, for dusting

1 Beat together the egg whites, confectioners' sugar, and flour, then mix in the butter.
2 Spoon two small spoonfuls of the batter (about 1½ tsp each) on a baking sheet lined with parchment paper. Smooth into thin oblongs measuring about 1½×8 inches.
3 Bake in a preheated 425°F oven until golden brown, 3–4 minutes. *Immediately* remove from the paper using a metal spatula and loosely roll each one around a wooden spoon handle. Once set, carefully remove from the spoon handle, place on a wire rack, and let cool completely.
4 Repeat until all the batter is used up, making about 24 tuiles. Once cold, place the tuiles in a well-sealed rigid container with parchment paper between the layers. Store for up to a week.
5 Dust the tuiles with confectioners' sugar before serving.

Chocolate Nut Bars

½ cup (1 stick) butter or margarine,
softened
5 tbsp sugar
¼ cup dark brown sugar, firmly
packed
¼ tsp salt
1 tsp vanilla extract
¾ cup self-rising flour
¾ cup rolled oats
1 egg

For the topping
3 oz semisweet or milk chocolate
⅓ cup sliced almonds

1 Grease a shallow cake pan measuring about 7 × 11 inches and line the bottom with wax paper. Cream together the butter, sugars, salt, and vanilla until pale and fluffy. Sift in the flour, then add the oats and the egg. Beat everything together thoroughly.

2 Spread the batter in the prepared pan and level the surface. Bake in a preheated 350°F oven until well risen, lightly browned, and shrinking away from the sides of the pan, about 25 minutes. Unmold and let cool on a wire rack.

3 Melt the chocolate (see page 12) and spread evenly on top of the cake. Sprinkle with the almonds and let set. Using a sharp knife, cut into about 16 bars.

Double Chocolate Chunk Cookies

These are real chocolate-packed cookies. Don't be surprised at the proportion of cookie dough to chocolate – it is correct!

4 tbsp butter or margarine, softened
5 tbsp sugar
¼ cup light brown sugar, firmly
packed
½ tsp vanilla extract
1 egg
¾ cup all-purpose flour
¼ tsp baking soda
¼ tsp salt
1 cup semisweet chocolate chips
6 oz white chocolate, chopped into
large chunks
¼ cup shelled unsalted pistachio
nuts

1 Cream the butter until very soft. Add all the remaining ingredients, except the pistachios, and mix thoroughly.

2 Put about 14 large spoonfuls of the dough, spaced well apart, on two large greased baking sheets. Press a few pistachio nuts into each spoonful. Bake in a preheated 350°F oven until the cookies are lightly tinged with brown, 10–12 minutes. Do not overcook the cookies; they should be soft in the center. Leave on the baking sheets to cool 10 minutes, then serve warm or transfer to wire racks and let cool completely.

EASY CHOCOLATE CAKE

A children's favorite!

SERVES 8

4 oz semisweet or milk chocolate
1 tbsp light corn syrup
½ cup (1 stick) butter or margarine
4 oz graham crackers, roughly broken up
3 tbsp raisins
3 tbsp candied cherries, halved
⅔ cup sliced almonds, toasted

1 Butter a 6- to 7-inch tart pan with a removable base or a springform cake pan.
2 Melt the chocolate (see page 12) with the syrup and butter.
3 When the chocolate mixture has melted, let it cool slightly before stirring in the remaining ingredients.
4 Turn the mixture into the prepared pan, lightly level the top, and chill until set.

CHOCOLATE SHORTIES

Sprinkling the grated chocolate on the cookies as soon as they come out of the oven ensures that it sticks.

MAKES ABOUT 3 DOZEN

1 cup + 6 tbsp self-rising flour
⅔ cup sugar
¼ tsp grated nutmeg
10 tbsp butter or margarine
1⅓ cups ground almonds
2 oz bittersweet chocolate, coarsely grated
1 egg, beaten

1 Grease three baking sheets. Sift the flour, sugar, and nutmeg into a bowl, then cut in the butter until the mixture resembles fine crumbs. Stir in the ground almonds and half the grated chocolate. Add the egg and mix together to form a dough.
2 Divide the dough in half and roll each piece on a sheet of wax paper or parchment paper into a 12-inch long thin sausage shape.
3 Chill in the freezer about 30 minutes or until firm.
4 Cut each roll at an angle into about 18 slices and place well apart on the prepared baking sheets. Bake in a preheated 375°F oven 15–20 minutes. Sprinkle with the remaining grated chocolate, then transfer to wire racks and let cool.

CHAPTER EIGHT

SAUCES,
AND
FROSTINGS

BUTTER FROSTING

Butter frosting can be used as a filling and to cover a cake

MAKES 9 OZ

6 tbsp butter, softened
1½ cups confectioners' sugar
a few drops of vanilla extract
1–2 tbsp milk or warm water

1 Put the butter in a bowl and cream until very soft. Sift and gradually beat in the confectioners' sugar, then add the vanilla and milk or water.
2 Spread the butter frosting using a metal or rubber spatula. Decorate by making swirls in the frosting or by marking with the tines of a fork. Butter frosting can also be piped.

Variations

Chocolate Dissolve 1 tbsp unsweetened cocoa powder in a little hot water and let cool before adding to the mixture.
Mocha Dissolve 1 tsp unsweetened cocoa powder and 2 tsp instant coffee granules in a little hot water taken from the measured amount. Let cool before adding to the mixture.
Orange or Lemon Replace the vanilla extract with a little finely grated orange or lemon rind. Add a little juice from the fruit instead of the milk, beating well to avoid curdling the mixture.
Coffee Replace the vanilla extract with 2 tsp instant coffee granules dissolved in some of the warm liquid; let cool before adding to the mixture. Or replace 1 tbsp of the liquid with the same amount of coffee flavoring.
Almond Add 2 tbsp finely chopped toasted almonds and mix thoroughly.

PERFECT CHOCOLATE GANACHE

This is the easiest and most foolproof method of making ganache, kindly taught to us by an experienced chocolatier. Use the very best chocolate for a really intense, bittersweet chocolate flavor.

Chocolate ganache is wonderfully versatile. Use it warm as a sauce for ice cream or poached pears, and whenever a rich chocolate sauce is called for. If lightly chilled, chocolate ganache will thicken, when it can be used as a filling for meringues, cakes, or cream puffs.

SERVES ABOUT 8

14 oz couverture chocolate or
11 oz bittersweet chocolate (see
Note)
1¼ cups heavy whipping cream

1 Using a large sharp knife, chop the chocolate into fairly small pieces and put it in a large heatproof bowl. Put the cream in a heavy-based saucepan and bring to a boil. Watch the cream carefully because it will rise up the pan and bubble over as it boils.
2 As soon as the cream boils, pour it over the chocolate. Leave, undisturbed, 5 minutes.
3 Using a large balloon whisk, begin whisking the mixture gently, starting from the center of the bowl and gradually incorporating all of the melted chocolate from the bottom. Serve while warm as a sauce, or let cool and thicken and use as a filling.

Note

When using couverture chocolate it is possible to use a higher proportion of chocolate to cream because melted couverture is more viscous than "ordinary" chocolate.

CHOCOLATE CUSTARD SAUCE

An everyday chocolate sauce to serve with steamed and baked puddings, pies, and cakes.

MAKES 1¼ CUPS

1 tbsp unsweetened cocoa powder
1½ tbsp cornstarch
about 1½ tbsp sugar, or to taste
1¼ cups milk

1 Blend the cocoa powder, cornstarch, and sugar to a smooth paste with a little of the milk.
2 In a heavy-based, preferably non-stick, saucepan, heat the remaining milk until almost boiling. Pour onto the cocoa mixture, stirring all the time. Return the mixture to the saucepan and bring to a boil, stirring constantly. Continue cooking 2 minutes after the sauce has boiled. Add a little extra sugar to taste, if desired. Serve the sauce hot.

Variations
Chocolate-Orange Custard Sauce Add the finely grated rind of 1 orange.
Coffee Custard Sauce Replace the cocoa powder with instant coffee granules.

CHOCOLATE FUDGE SAUCE

Serve this sticky fudge sauce with profiteroles, ice cream, and bananas. In winter, add a tablespoonful of rum, brandy, or liqueur to the finished sauce.

MAKES ABOUT 2 CUPS

⅓ cup light whipping cream
⅓ cup unsweetened cocoa powder
½ cup + 1 tbsp sugar
½ cup light corn syrup
2 tbsp butter or margarine
a pinch of salt
½ tsp vanilla extract

1 Combine all the ingredients, except the vanilla, in a saucepan over low heat and mix well. Slowly bring to a boil, stirring occasionally. Boil 5 minutes, then add the vanilla.
2 Let the hot fudge sauce cool slightly before serving.

CHOCOLATE NUT BUTTER

Serve with hot pancakes and waffles or on toast.

SERVES 4

½ cup (1 stick) butter, softened
2 tsp sugar
2 tbsp grated chocolate
2 tbsp finely chopped walnuts,
hazelnuts, or pecans

Beat the butter until very light and fluffy, then beat in the remaining ingredients.

STIRRED EGG CUSTARD

This is a lightly thickened "real" custard sauce, and makes a good accompaniment for some of our more special chocolate desserts. It's also the base for rich, creamy bavarian (set custard) and wonderful ice creams. It should be silky smooth with no sign of curdling, so it must never boil. It can be made in a double boiler, but this is very slow. If you're careful using a saucepan, you'll have perfect custard every time.

SERVES 4

½ vanilla bean
1¼ cups milk
3 egg yolks
4 tsp sugar

1 Split open the vanilla bean and scrape out the seeds into a medium, heavy-based saucepan. Add the bean and the milk. Bring slowly to a boil, take off the heat, cover, and let infuse 30 minutes. Remove the vanilla bean.
2 Place the egg yolks and sugar in a medium bowl. Using a balloon whisk, electric mixer, or wooden spoon, beat the yolks and sugar until they lighten in color and thicken slightly.
3 Pour the infused milk onto the mixture, whisking or stirring until evenly mixed. Rinse the saucepan, then return the mixture to the pan. Have ready a cold bowl with a strainer over the top.
4 Place the saucepan over low to medium heat and cook the custard, stirring all the time, until it thickens slightly and begins to coat the back of the spoon, about 10 minutes. Do not boil or the custard will curdle. (Watch the froth on the custard – when it begins to disappear, the custard is starting to thicken.)
5 Immediately strain the custard into the cold bowl to stop it cooking further. Whisk to reduce the temperature. To serve warm, pour into a pitcher. To serve cold, place damp parchment paper on the surface of the hot custard to prevent a skin from forming, let cool, and then chill.

Variations
Chocolate Omit the vanilla bean. Break up 2 ounces bittersweet chocolate and bring it slowly to a boil with the milk, whisking until smooth. Complete as above, using 1 tbsp sugar only.
Orange, Lemon, or Mint Omit the vanilla bean. Add the pared rind of ½ lemon or ½ orange, or a handful of washed mint, to the milk and bring to a boil. Complete as above, straining the milk onto the egg yolks.
Nutmeg and Sherry Omit the vanilla bean. Prepare the custard as above, adding a pinch of grated nutmeg and 1–2 tbsp sherry wine at the end.
Extra Creamy Replace half or all of the milk with light whipping cream, or half light and half heavy cream.

Notes
It is important to rinse out the saucepan in step 3 before heating the mixture, to avoid the custard burning onto the bottom of the pan. If the custard begins to separate and look like runny scrambled eggs, it is curdling. To rescue it, strain it immediately into the cold bowl, add a few ice cubes, and whisk vigorously to reduce the temperature – it should smooth out again quite quickly. If you are nervous about curdling the custard, beat 1 tsp cornstarch with the egg yolks in step 2. This helps thicken the custard, but taste it after cooking to ensure that all traces of cornstarch flavor have disappeared. If necessary, stir over very low heat for a little longer, but do not boil.
For convenience, a few drops of vanilla extract can replace the vanilla bean. Add to the milk at the beginning of step 3.

RASPBERRY COULIS

This fruity, vivid pink sauce is delicious with all manner of chocolate concoctions, and of course it's obligatory when serving a dessert "nouvelle" style. We particularly liked it with Chocolate Roulade (see page 86), Chocolate Heaven (see page 106), or White Chocolate and Sherry Mousse (see page 97) and almost any frozen chocolate pudding. Don't be tempted to add too much sugar; remember that the chocolate mixture is likely to be quite sweet.

SERVES 4

8 oz fresh raspberries
confectioners' sugar, to taste
a splash of your favorite liqueur
(optional)

1 Purée the raspberries in a blender or food processor, then push through a nylon strainer to remove the seeds. If the raspberries are very ripe, it may be possible simply to push them through a strainer to purée them.
2 Add confectioners' sugar to taste, then stir in a little liqueur, if using. Serve cold.

FRESH ORANGE SAUCE

Serve with Double Chocolate Ice Cream (see page 113). Blood oranges give the best color.

SERVES 4

6 oranges, preferably blood oranges
2 tsp cornstarch
2 tbsp sugar

1 With a swivel-bladed peeler, thinly pare the rind from one orange and set aside. Squeeze the juice from all the oranges into a measuring cup and add water to make 1¼ cups if necessary. Strain into a small saucepan. Blend the cornstarch to a smooth paste with 2 tbsp water and stir into the orange juice with the sugar.
2 Bring the sauce slowly to a boil, stirring constantly. Simmer until slightly thickened and clear, then pour into a bowl, cover loosely, and set aside to cool.
3 Cut the reserved orange rind into needle-thin shreds. Drop into a saucepan of boiling water and simmer until tender, 3–4 minutes. Drain and cool under cold water, then add to the sauce. Serve cold.

BUTTER CREAM

Use this rich butter cream to fill chocolate cakes, particularly rolled ones.

MAKES ABOUT 10 OZ

7 tbsp sugar
2 egg yolks, beaten
¾ cup (1½ sticks) butter, softened

1 Place the sugar in a heavy-based saucepan, add ¼ cup water, and heat very gently to dissolve the sugar, without boiling.
2 When the sugar is completely dissolved, bring to a boil and boil steadily 2–3 minutes, to reach a temperature of 225°F. (Check the temperature on a candy thermometer.)
3 Pour the syrup in a thin stream onto the egg yolks in a deep bowl, beating all the time. Continue to beat until the mixture is thick and cold.
4 In another bowl, cream the butter until very soft, then gradually beat in the egg yolk mixture.

Variations

Chocolate Melt 2 oz bittersweet chocolate with 1 tbsp water (see page 14). Let cool slightly and beat into the butter cream.
Fruit Crush 8 oz fresh strawberries, raspberries, etc., or thaw, drain, and crush frozen fruit. Beat into the butter cream.
Orange or Lemon Add freshly grated rind and juice to taste to the butter cream.
Coffee Beat 1–2 tbsp coffee flavoring into the butter cream.

CHOCOLATE FUDGE FROSTING

MAKES ENOUGH TO FILL AND COVER THE TOP OF AN 8-INCH CAKE

4 tbsp butter
½ cup light brown sugar, firmly packed
3 oz semisweet chocolate, broken into pieces
2 tbsp cream
1¾ cups confectioners' sugar, sifted

1 Put the butter, brown sugar, chocolate, and cream in a saucepan.
2 Heat gently until the sugar has dissolved, then bring to a boil and boil briskly 3 minutes.
3 Remove from the heat and gradually stir in the confectioners' sugar. Beat until smooth, using a wooden spoon, and continue to beat until the frosting is thick enough to spread, about 2 minutes. Use immediately, spreading with a wet metal spatula.

SEVEN-MINUTE FROSTING

MAKES ABOUT 6 OZ

1 egg white
¾ cup sugar
a pinch of salt
a pinch of cream of tartar

1 Put the ingredients in a heatproof bowl with 2 tbsp water. Beat lightly.
2 Set the bowl over a pan of hot water and beat until the mixture thickens sufficiently to stand in peaks. This will take about 7 minutes.
3 Pour the frosting over the top of the cake and spread with a metal spatula.

ACKNOWLEDGMENTS

We would like to thank the following: Carrie Groom of the Porter Chocolate Company for her help and words of wisdom; Moyra Fraser, Caroline Walker, Fiona Hunter, Riley Stemp, Sarah Edmunds, Kate Fryer, Carla Newman, and Camilla Stevens for forgetting their diets for the duration of the recipe testing; Helen Casey for being a great help and Sylvia Stephenson.
We would also like to thank James Murphy, Roísín Nield, Tom, and Nat for the yummy photographs, and Sander Architectural Mirrors, Sander House, Elmore Street, London N1.
Finally, special thanks to Julia Thorpe.

INDEX